John Barnes was born within 300 yards of the Liverpool Kop and spent his formative years in the rural setting of South Yorkshire. Still living in the same area with his wife, Pauline, children, Joanne and Jonathan, and grandchildren, Lola, Camilla, Lucia and Troy living close by, he is now in the twilight of his career as a director of several companies and was inspired to write his first book at the age of 62, with a lifetime of adventures and experiences.

To family and friends without whom life would be very boring.

John F Barnes

IF ONLY...

AUSTIN MACAULEY PUBLISHERS™

LONDON * CAMBRIDGE * NEW YORK * SHARJAH

A CIP catalogue record for this title is available from the British Library.

ISBN 9781398434837 (Paperback)
ISBN 9781398434844 (ePub e-book)

www.austinmacauley.com

First Published 2022
Austin Macauley Publishers Ltd®
1 Canada Square
Canary Wharf
London
E14 5AA

I have been extremely fortunate to have met and remain lifelong friends with so many humorous and charismatic people who have inspired many of the funny situations, adventures and experiences that are contained within If Only.

Whilst the majority of the content just flowed, my first thanks are to my wife, Pauline, firstly, for being at my side for 45 years, and secondly, for also reminding me of several adventures that are contained within the book.

I met Lee Metterick and Dave Carney when I was eight years old and we have remained best friends to this day. Many of the adventures and experiences were with them.

Dave's dad, Alf, being a typical comical scouser led us up the garden path with many of his tall stories.

Roy Conway was my partner in crime during our late teens in Leeds, and then along came Neil Albert Podmore, initially as a team-mate, then a friend and work colleague and possibly one of the funniest characters anyone could meet, he has many contributions within the book.

I have spent a lot of time over the past 30 years playing football, and on both skiing and sun holidays, with Adrian Hawkins (AKA African Sunset), and many of the funny experiences have found their way into the book.

My brother in law john Wilson (fat Jonny) was the brunt of a funny practical joke but to be fair he more than received his revenge on me with both forming part of the story.

Finally, a mention for big Dave. Sanders, unfortunately, no longer with us, who was a massive character, and Roy Jackson, who might well be one of the most humorous guys I have ever met, but, unfortunately, has only one contribution to the book!

Chapter One

James Burgess (Budgie), Ryan Fletcher (Fletch) and Michael Johnstone (Jono or Bugle, due to the size of his nose) got off the bus and headed for Yee's Chinese chip shop on Hardwick Main Street. They had been playing for the school team that morning and were starving.

James was the leader of the trio for several reasons, his strong personality, cheeky smile that endeared most people he came into contact with, athletic prowess for almost 16-year-old and the fact he was captain of most of the teams he played in.

He wasn't the fizziest drink in the fridge when it came to academics, although he was no dummy either and despite this he had been chosen 'head of year' for his overall persona.

The three lived in a relatively small village called, Hardwick which was considered 'posh' by the neighbouring villages.

It was 1974 and most villages in South Yorkshire were centred around a coalmine and the sky line was dominated by a slag heap and the large wheel on top of the mine that took the men down by to the coal face.

Hardwick had no coalmine and was made up of a number of small estates of bungalows and semi-detached houses with a spine of 'posh houses' on the main road out of the village. The hub was the row of shops in the centre where most of the teenagers congregated in their free time.

They entered the Chinese chippy. "Hi, Yee, you okay?" asked Budgie as they walked in to the shop which always smelled the same a mixture of fish, smelly socks and stale tobacco from the clientele the previous evening.

Yee was standing behind the counter wearing his usual white overall that over the years had turned more of a yellow and looked like it hadn't been washed for a while. He had a grin which showed his two rows of teeth that were of a similar colour. He was about 5ft 3 inches and could only just see over the counter.

Him and his wife, Dongmie, ran the shop working from 11am to 11pm, seven days a week, and they could have been anywhere between 30 and 50 years old.

The boys went in on a regular basis and enjoyed the mickey taking and banter, not sure Yee felt the same way, but he joined in and welcomed the custom.

"Okay boys, you wah fish?" he asked.

"No fish today, Yee," replied Budgie. "Just three lots of chips and two large curries, please."

"If you wah fish, if so I need fly."

"No, Yee," replied Jono, "we said no wah fish and no wan flies!"

Yee scowled at the comment. "Okay boy, I only ask."

Eventually, he shovelled out three potions of chips.

Yee slopped two curries into cartons, in between he wiped his nose on the back of his hand.

"You wah sore a finger?" asked Yee.

"Loads of sore fingers please, Yee," answered Jono.

"Wapped or open?" he asked.

"Wapped," replied Jono.

He bagged the goods and handed them over.

"You always cheeky boys," said Yee. "I speak good Engwish, and better than you do Chinese, and when China takes over, we see how well you speak my wanguage."

"Well when they do, I will order sweet and sour pok with flied lice, but until then, its good old British food and English language for us," said James.

"Ha, you boys also stupid and cheeky cos cuwwy no Bwitish!"

The three lads smiled, paid the money and left.

"He's hard work, that Yee," said Jono, "but he has got a point, I can't speak Chinese and god knows how they understand that Chinese writing, they must be brainy just to remember all them funny symbols."

"You're right about being clever, but he needs to smarten himself up when it comes to hygiene," replied Fletch.

"He makes good curry to be fair though, it has a kick on it like an aborigine's armpit," said Jono.

"How do you know what an aborigine arm pit is like?" asked Fetch.

"Well, they live where it is 40 degrees and I don't think they have many showers in the outback so it's just a guess," replied Jono.

"Good point," said Budgie, "come on, we'll take these back to ours, get some bread and butter and a cup of tea and watch on the ball." (The football programme that preceded the 3 o'clock kick offs.)

"Sounds good to me, mate," they said in unison.

They walked into the living room to find Peter, James' dad, sitting in the armchair wearing tracksuit bottoms and an off-white vest, with a copy of *The Sporting Life* on his lap.

"Aye, aye, it's the Busby babes, how did you get on, lads?" Peter asked.

"Won three nil," replied James. "Jono scored two."

"Your James levelled their centre forward as well, Mr Burgess," said Fletch.

"He was getting too gobby for his own good, so I gave him a steadier when everyone was looking the other way," said James.

Peter laughed. "If I gave you a steadier every time you got too gobby, son, you would be permanent black and blue by now," he said.

"Well you've missed your chance 'cos you're not hard enough now, Father."

In a flash, Peter jumped up and got James in a bear hug, squeezing the wind out of him.

"Dad, you're hurting me," squealed James.

Ryan and Michael burst out laughing seeing their big, tough mate begging for mercy.

Peter sat back down. "Still got it, son," he said. "Still got it."

"Where's me mum?" asked James.

Gone to the bingo with Betty from next door, and I have got three hours of peace and quiet and watching the racing on tele.

The lads made their way to the kitchen, James made the tea, Fletch buttered the bread and Jono set the table.

Fletch and Jono had been coming into the Burgess house since they were in primary school so they knew their way around the kitchen.

They all sat down to eat and watch the build up to the day's games.

"How come you're not doing a foreigner?" asked James.

"I was doing, but they cancelled this morning, they had to go out or something and I am glad now it's started raining."

"Listen, do me a favour when you've finished your dinner, I've already put a yankee on but I fancy an outsider in the 2 o' clock so nip to the bookies and put me a bet on," said Peter.

"You're not putting your money on another donkey they've dragged off Blackpool beach are you, Dad?"

"Listen, this is a racing certainty but 20 to 1 so I'm backing it each way."

Peter turned to Michael. "Talking of donkeys," he said, "do you know what I read in the paper this morning? They've got camels on Blackpool beach nowadays as well as donkeys. Can you believe that?"

"Have they, Mr Burgess?"

"Yep, and do you know what they have for their dinner?"

"No, what?" asked Jono.

"Thirty minutes the same as the donkeys." With that, he burst out laughing. "Thirty minutes the same as the donkeys!" Peter always had to say the punch line twice.

Jono laughed out of respect and Fletch smiled but shook his head.

"That's pathetic," said James.

They cleared their plates and Peter wrote out his bet on a piece of paper that he folded twice. He got 50p from his pocket.

"Right, son, be quick. It's off soon. Just tell Bob the bookie behind the counter it's for me, you'll be fine."

"He'll know I wouldn't put my money on donkeys like that," replied James as he took the paper and money.

"Quick boys, you had better hurry up because if you miss the start, you're standing the bet."

I might stand it anyway because I would rather have the money than give it to Bob the bookie, said James.

As they set off towards the high street, Jono asked, "You really going to stand the bet?"

"No, better not, it would be just my luck it came in and I would owe him a fortune."

They got to the bookies. Fletch and Jono stayed outside the bookies and James walked up to the counter.

"My dad's asked me to put this bet on for him, Bob, but it's probably no chance as usual."

Bob took the paper and opened it. He shook his head and shouted over to the man sitting in front of the racing papers on the wall. "Stan, there's a horse in the two o' clock at Kempton with the second name 'Hearted'—I can't quite read the first name."

Stan pulled his glasses down from his forehead. "Nothing in the first race ending in 'Hearted'," he shouted over.

"Must be, have another look," said Bob.

"No definitely nothing ending in hearted," said Stan.

"Oh, hold on, the first name is 'Hoof,' as in 'horse's hoof'."

Stan looked again. "No, nothing starting with the word 'hoof'," he said.

"Are you sure?" asked Bob.

"Yep," said Stan. "There's no horse running called Hoof Hearted in the two o'clock."

Everyone in the bookies burst out laughing.

"Check the two o'clock at Redcar?" requested Bob.

"No," said Stan. "No Hoof Hearted running there either."

The clientele and Bill were doubled up with laughter, James realised he had been set up.

"I think the joke's on you, son," said Bob, handing him back the paper and the money.

"I think the joke's on him 'cos he can whistle for getting his 50p," said James, as he picked up the money and the paper from the counter and walked to the door.

"Close that door on the way out, Jimbo," said Bob. "I think the wind's getting up."

"Yes, we don't want it blowing off in here," shouted one of the customers, sparking another round of cackles.

James turned around and stuck two fingers up to the lot of them and walked out, leaving the door wide open.

As he walked out, Jono and Fletch were talking to Beverly Lewis and her mate, Sharon. Beverly looked stunning in a crop top and short skirt.

"Aren't you cold?" asked James.

"I'm always hot, James," she replied with a grin.

James blushed at the reply. Apart from Fletch, James and his mates were still into football and girls were only just starting to figure on their agenda.

They were village lads at heart and not as street wise as most 16-year lads from the cities.

"Have you put the bet on?" asked Jono.

"Don't even go there, he chuffing set me up, didn't he? But I'm keeping the 50p." He passed over the bet and Jono read it out, "25 p each way, Hoof hearted in the two o'clock at Kempton." Everyone laughed including the girls and even James managed a grin at the set up.

"I will get my own back on the old bugger," he said.

The lads said their goodbyes to the girls and as they walked off, Fletch shouted back, "See you tomorrow!" The lads thought this strange but didn't think any more about it.

"She's a babe, that Beverly," said Fletch. "They both agreed but apart from Fletch, they thought she was out of their league."

"What are we gonna do for the rest of the day?" asked Jono.

"Don't know, but when I go in for tea, I'm staying in," replied James. "Going to have a soak in the bath. I feel a bit stiff and we play Manton tomorrow, so I want to be fit."

"You're right, mate. Billy will be on our backs if we're all not up for it tomorrow."

They hung around the shops for a while and were joined by Paul Lemington, Lemmy and Neil Hawksworth, Ginners, Ginge, or plain Ginger, due to his bright ginger hair. It wouldn't have been so obvious if he had it cut short but it was long, curly and frizzy like an Afro. He had recently seen an advertisement poster in a hair dressing saloon for a hair die company showing a gorgeous woman with red flowing hair stating, choose your hair to be 'African sunset'. Since then, Neil continually tried to convince everyone he wasn't Ginger he was African Sunset but they were having none of it.

The talk was mainly of the Manton game tomorrow and as it started to rain once again one by one, they drifted off home.

James arrived home to find Mum, Dad and Alex, his younger brother, having tea and corned beef hash with baked beans, James' favourite.

"Yours is in the oven," his mum said.

"How did my bet go on?" enquired his dad with a grin from ear to ear.

"It lost," replied James as he walked into the kitchen.

"What do you mean it lost?"

"I put the bet on with Bob the bookie as you said and we listened to the commentary, but it was never mentioned, must have come last or fallen, one of the two."

"What do you mean it wasn't mentioned? Of course, it wasn't mentioned."

"I don't know what you mean, Dad, I put the bet on as you asked and that was the last, I heard of it."

James sat down to his favourite meal and poured brown sauce over the top.

"Come on, hand it over," demanded his dad.

James reached for his pocket and pulled out the piece of paper the bet had been written on which he had previously torn it into a hundred pieces.

"Dad, all I can say is that what happened to Hoof Hearted in the two o' clock and the 50p bet will remain a mystery forever because the answer, my friend, is blowing in the wind, the answer is blowing in the wind." With that, he blew the torn pieces of paper towards his dad. He was referring to the song by his dad's favourite singer, Bob Dylan.

Peter looked at Sheila and then at Alex who both had their heads down trying not to laugh. James carried on with his tea with a smile on his face but didn't dare look at his father.

Sheila started clearing up the dinner dishes and walked into the kitchen as she burst out laughing.

"Think it's back fired this time, Pete," she said as she came back in.

"It will back fire on him if he doesn't hand it over."

James said nothing but carried on with his tea savouring the moment and certain it wasn't getting handed back.

Chapter Two

The next morning, it was typically cold for March and Billy Steele was about to give his talk to the Hardwick lads before announcing the team. Billy was an ex-pro in the lower leagues and when his career was over, he desperately wanted to continue into management. Despite gaining all his badges and being the perfect manager, he didn't draw the attention of club chairman (he always felt if he had an Italian or Spanish name it might have been different), so he settled for a job in insurance and managing a good non-league team on Saturdays and his local village under-16 team on Sunday mornings as he had brought the set of lads through since under 14s. His record with both clubs was good and he lived in hope that one day he would get his chance. Billy was a scouser and whilst he had lived in for Yorkshire for 30 years, he still had a faint scouse accent which came out even stronger when he was getting irate on the touch line. He didn't want to be called Mr Steele or Billy, for that matter, so he insisted the lads refer to him as 'gaffer' which is what he had called all his managers through the years.

The 15 lads sat around the perimeter of the changing room on benches, quietly waiting for the talk and to see if they had been selected. There was a tall blond skinny lad sitting in the corner. No one had seen him before. He didn't particularly look the football type, but the lad sat there with an air of confidence. The team looked at him and nodded but didn't speak. They assumed he had come into the wrong changing room or was just a mate of one of the team members.

They were playing a mining village, Manton rovers from the other side of town, and they knew it would be a physical game. They were the type of team that would rather have a massive brawl to upset and intimidate the opposition rather than play good football but Hardwick knew if they just played to their strengths and stuck to the game plan they should win comfortably.

"Right, lads listen up, we cannot afford any slip ups today, four games left and if we win all four, we win the league," said Billy Steele. "You know Manton aren't in our class but if we don't match them in the tackle, they will take us to the cleaners. Main aim is to pass the ball to feet, keep possession and attack them on the wings, we know their full backs are big meat heads but slow."

Mickey his assistant stood by his side and nodded and repeated certain poignant words.

James sat quietly knowing as team captain, he was almost certainly in the side. He was the engine room in the middle of the pitch and Billy had made him captain because of his leadership skills, his endless energy, and also, to try and calm him down. Whilst James was not generally the aggressive type, sometimes when he was between two sets of goal posts, football or rugby or in front of a batsman, a mist would come over him and he would lose it. Every ref knew him due to his quality of play and because most had booked him over the years.

Hardwick was made up of 6 players from the village the remainder being quality players from surrounding villages and they were a tight bunch of lads who had been mainly been together since under 14s.

"Right," said Billy, "I realise there are only four games left, but I have brought along Paul Croft." He pointed over to the blond-haired lad, who put his hand up. "He actually signed for us at start of the season but has been with Leeds academy and ineligible to play. They have finished their league now and he has permission to play for us. I know that may seem unfair bringing him in at this late stage but it's best for the team."

The lads didn't take kindly to outsiders, especially ones that looked like they should be in a boy band not on a football pitch. Most gave him a slight glare, but he kept looking around the room and didn't seem notice or care what they thought.

The minute the team was named, the changing room erupted and they scrambled for the best kit.

"Listen, lads, I want you forwards to play your heart out 'cos I am going to pull one of you off at half time and bring on Crofty for the second half."

"Bloody hell," said Crofty, "the manager's going to pull you off, we only got an orange at half time at Leeds."

The lads burst out laughing and he was halfway to winning them over. Once changed, Billy instructed them to get the nets and corner flags out of the store.

"Ginner, you get on Clanger's shoulders and tie the nets up."

Clanger was the keeper, the tallest lad on the team and aptly nicknamed Clanger due to the goal keeping mishaps he had made since he became a keeper six years ago.

"I pity you," said Ginner. "I had the curry from Yee's last night and I've got an arse like a bird's nest this morning, all shit and twigs."

The changing room erupted into laughter with a great description of how his arse might look, full of shit and twigs.

"You're not going on my shoulders then, you little twat," said Clanger.

"Shut up," shouted Budgie. "You've got shit for brains, so what's a bit more around your neck?"

The laughter rang out again.

"Come on, lads," shouted Billy. "Fifteen minutes to kick off!"

"Come on," they all shouted in unison as they left the home dressing room, mainly to let the away team know they were up for it.

The game went as predicted with Hardwick having most of the possession and Manton reverting to intimidation and fouls as they felt the game slipping away. Hardwick went two up before half time.

Billy changed the format for the second half, going 433 instead of 442 now they had the slope of the pitch in their favour. The second half started with the flat-nosed thug at left back tackling Jono, who had made him look an idiot on several occasions in the first half. A fight immediately broke out between five players and several supporters came onto the pitch. The ref finally resumed order and the game restarted without the full back who had received a red card much to the pleasure of Jono.

"Get warmed up, Stubby," shouted Billy to Jack Stubbs, one of the substitutes.

"About time you brought me on," Stubby shouted back.

"No, you're not going on," replied Billy, "You're looking cold so get warmed up!"

The side-line burst out laughing and this together with the embarrassment caused Stubby to say, "Piss off, you tosser," just loud enough for Billy to hear and something he regretted as he immediately realised it ruined his chances of getting on.

The match finished 3-0 with Crofty coming on as sub, scoring a twenty-five yarder and showing why he was on Leeds books.

The mood was electric in the changing room afterwards. They piled into the showers which were only lukewarm, but the muddy knees and hands were in desperate need of washing. As usual, Banksy came out of the showers dripping wet but his hair a dry as a bone. He had the fashionable Kevin Keegan curly hair which he claimed was natural and he wasn't getting that wet for anyone.

The lads tried to splash him, but he wasn't having any and made a getaway for the changing rooms to the shouts of all the lads. Despite there not being a hair out of place, he spent five minutes in front of the mirror making sure all the curls were perfect.

Billy gave his usual debrief and finished by reminding them it was away next Sunday against the bottom side and to meet at 9.30am outside the shops.

Budgie, Jono and Fletch walked home together, they had done most things together for the past ten years.

"That Crofty is a good player," said Fletch.

"Different gravy," replied Jono.

"I agree, but he's just the type to get out of the bath to have a piss," said James.

"Budgie, are you saying you can't be bothered to get out of the bath to have a slash?" asked Fletch.

"Not in winter I don't get out no, we've not got central heating in our house and it's freezing."

"Urgh," said Jono. "Fancy having a bath in your own pee."

"I feel sorry for our Alex, he has to follow me," added James, "it's a wonder he hasn't turned yellow by now."

They all laughed at the thought of poor Alex sat in the bath unaware of the ingredients.

"What you doing tonight?" asked Fletch.

"Shagging Beverly Lewis if she plays her cards right, I'm meeting her at 5.00 tonight."

"Why didn't you tell us about this yesterday?" enquired James.

"Just in case she didn't turn up but I think she's up for it big time."

Everyone knew Beverly Lewis was the best-looking girl in the year, including Beverly Lewis, so they were impressed that Fletch had the guts to ask her out. Jono and Budgie were jealous but didn't show it.

"You haven't got a shag in you," said Jono.

"Least I'm not still a virgin," replied Fletch.

"You kidding?" said Jono.

"Tell him, Budgie. You were at that party where I took Diane Sayles upstairs two weeks ago, I gave her a right seeing to."

"The only thing I can remember is you going upstairs with her and two minutes later she came back down on her own. Apparently, you came in your underpants before you got to the top of the stairs."

"She said that?"

"The lying bitch! I gave her two minutes she will remember for the rest of her life," Jono replied.

All three laughed and said their goodbyes before they went their separate ways.

Chapter Three

James' home life was good, they were a close family who enjoyed the banter which flowed between the four males and occasionally from Sheila, who had had to learn how to stand her ground being the only female in the house but she could give as good as she got.

James had two brothers, Neville who was three years older and a trainee mechanic in the local garage and Alex who was a total surprise to Peter and Sheila, came along five years after James. Alex being the baby of the family got away with things his brothers would never have and as so much rubbed off from his older brothers he was ahead of his age compared to his mates.

Money was tight however despite Nev now working and paying a bit of board. His mother unbeknown to his dad usually gave most of it back knowing he was an apprentice and not earning good money and had just bought a ford Capri and most of his wages went on the monthly payments. They lived in a three-bedroom semi which meant James had to share a bedroom with Alex. Peter had worked himself up from the tools to be a foreman brick layer and then up to site foreman and Sheila worked in the kitchen at the local primary school, 5 hours a day.

James walked into the front room to find Nev and Alex watching TV, his mum was in the kitchen cooking Sunday lunch.

"How did you get on?" asked Nev.

"Won three nil," replied James. "All kicked off as usual you know what Manton are like."

"Trust me I know, don't take any prisoners them boys, I was going to come down, but had a skin-full last night so I stayed in bed."

His mother came in with knives and forks as he said it.

"Yes. I heard you come in," she said. "Don't you have any consideration for others?"

"Me too," added Alex, "you woke me up banging and clattering."

"Listen if you can't have a drink on a Saturday night, when can you have a drink? Anyway I was only thinking of one thing, a cheese sarnie and then bed."

"Anyways," said James. "Make sure you're there for the last game of the season in three weeks it's Kivo away and bring your mates, too."

"Wouldn't miss that game against Kivo for the world, James, my little brother," said Nev.

Nev had had his run ins with Kivo, the local rivals over the years but a combination of an injured ankle a year ago, his girlfriend Karen, beer and having to work Saturdays meant he had hung his boots up earlier this season for the time being at least but he was a good footballer himself when fit.

Me, Snid and a few mates will be there as well James so if it kicks off we will wade in all guns blazing.

James, Nev and Pete burst out laughing at the thought of Alex and Snid verses the Kivo thugs.

Alex and Sid or Snid had been friends since nursery school but Alex could never pronounce properly his name Sidney and called him Snidney or Snid. The name stuck with everyone even his mum and dad at times.

Alex ignored the laughs. "What's for dinner, Mum?" he enquired.

"Chicken," replied Sheila, "I managed to bring home a few chicken breasts from school on Friday."

"Thank God it's not beef again, that meat you pinched from the school kitchen last week was so tough it threatened to take me outside and give me a good hiding," said Nev, "it's a wonder the kids didn't break all their teeth trying to chew it."

Sheila managed a smile at the comment. "Hey, I don't pinch this food. I only bring it home when it would be out of date anyway so someone may as well have the benefit."

"Listen, we're not complaining, and I bet all the kitchen staff do it."

"No comment," Sheila replied.

With that and right on time, the key could be heard in the front door and Peter came in clearly having quenched his thirst with his mates as he always did on Sunday lunchtime. He kissed Sheila on the side of the cheek and fell into his armchair.

Now that Alex was bigger, they struggled to get around the table when they were all at home and Peter had volunteered to have his on a tray whenever all the family were there. It also meant he could fall into his Sunday afternoon snooze without having to change chairs.

"My God you wreak of beer, Pete, how many have you had?" Sheila asked.

"Four pints, my sweet and I told Tommy the landlord he must put ground up sleeping tablets in his beer on a Sunday because no matter how I try I can't keep my eyes open after my Sunday dinner."

"I don't know how you get so thirsty, Dad," said Alex. "It's not like you do a lot of exercise."

"You will see me exercise in a minute when I get up and box your ears."

Sheila put a tray on his lap with a plate over-flowing with food.

"He's right you know, Pete. You're getting a right beer gut, you won't be able to fit that tray on your lap soon," said Sheila.

"He won't need a tray soon. Just rest his plate on his belly, it's getting like a shelf." Laughed Alex.

Peter ignored the comment and tucked in. Halfway through, he put his knife and fork down and said, "Hey Sheila, I got big Roy in the pub today. You know how big he is, his forearms are like my thighs."

"Anyway, he used to arm wrestle for money and he was telling the tale again today so I said to him, I used to be good at arm wrestling, but I don't keep going on about it."

He said, "You serious you think you can honestly arm wrestle me?"

I said, "Yes, I'll arm wrestle you for two quid."

He looked at me, laughed and said, "I know you're a big guy, Pete, but you're not in my league."

I said, "So you're bottling it, are you?"

To which he said, "You want to arm wrestle me for two quid?"

"Yep," I replied, "bring it on."

"Right, put your money and your elbow on the table." We both put our money down and everyone gathered around.

We locked hands and I tried my best for the first twenty seconds, but I knew he had me beat and he put me down. I picked the money up and said, "Cheers, pal, well done."

"Why did you do that if he won?" asked Alex.

"Funny you should ask that, son, 'cos that's what he said. I told him I would arm wrestle him for two quid, I didn't say I would beat him."

"What did he do then?" asked James.

"I don't know I supped up and left sharpish before he realised what I'd done and grabbed hold of me, he fell for that one." Peter chuckled over his food.

"I pity you next time he sees you, Dad," said Nev.

"He will have got over it by then, I hope anyway," replied Peter.

They finished their dinner and Sheila helped by James and Alex cleared up the dishes.

As Alex removed his tray, Peter announced, "Right, Sunday afternoon nap is fathers' privilege."

"Every day is fathers' privilege," responded Sheila as she was wiping the table.

"Listen, I am at work five days a week and then I do jobs on the side on Saturdays so I deserve a day off."

"So, when do I get a day's off?" asked Sheila.

"Well, I'm not being funny, my sweet, but you can't call it hard work peeling a few spuds and putting a few crosses on the bottom of the sprouts," he replied.

The dishcloth hit Peter on the side of the face hard and as it fell onto his shoulder, it left a residue of carrots, mashed potato and gravy on his cheek.

Peter never flinched and sat there with a smirk as well as the food on his face.

"Wipe that smirk off your face or I will get the rolling pin." Snapped Sheila.

"Surely you're not going to start baking at this time, are you, love?" Peter asked sarcastically.

Sheila spun around and made for the kitchen.

The sound of drawers opening and being slammed shut could be heard.

"I would scarper if I were you, dad, I think you have pushed her too far," said Alex.

Peter agreed, he grabbed the newspaper and ran upstairs as fast as his inebriated body would allow, he went into the bathroom and locked the door and sat on the toilet reading the paper for the next 30 minutes until he was sure it was safe to come out.

Chapter Four

Ryan Fletcher was a little more privileged than his mates, living in a nice detached house with his mum and dad. Ryan was an only child. He was an all-rounder, a cheeky personality and good at most sports and cleverer than he appeared at school, but he purposely held himself back, not wanting to alienate himself from his mates and preferring to be the class comedian. He knew this was something he may regret later in life, but at this moment, he had other priorities.

He had fancied Beverly Lewis for a while, who didn't, and had finally plucked up courage to ask her out the previous week. She couldn't make Saturday but agreed to meet him for a pizza on Sunday evening at the newly opened pizza place, Italian gardens. Bev had never had a pizza and so agreed to go. Ryan had several funny stories and jokes ready to impress and arrived at the newly opened pizza place at 4.45 pm. He paced up and down outside for the next hour, but Beverly didn't arrive.

He finally gave up and left for home at 5.45 with a pizza in its box, totally dejected and embarrassed that she had stood him up. As he walked home, he made himself a promise to have two-time rule. If he were let down like that, he would have his revenge twice over.

Ryan walked to get the school bus on the Monday morning and as he turned the corner and walked towards the bus stop, he saw Beverly stood with her mates all having a good laugh about something. They saw Ryan approaching and fell silent but the smirks remained. Ryan walked up with the saddest of faces. He stared at Beverly who looked stunning as always. As usual, she had left home and as soon as she turned the corner, she turned the waistband of her skirt over twice to make it look more like a belt than a skirt.

"Bev, I am so, so sorry," he said.

"What for?" she asked.

"My grandparents came around and not only did I completely lose track of time, but it wouldn't have been right to leave them. I hope you didn't wait for long?"

The smirk disappeared from her face, although remained on her friend's.

"You didn't turn up?" she asked.

"No, as I said, when they left and I realised what time it was, I was sure you would have gone by then."

"Well, I didn't waste any time 'cos I didn't turn up either."

Bev had changed her mind as she had always secretly admired James and was worried if she did meet Ryan, it would ruin her chances.

"Oh charming," he replied. "Thanks for that, what was your reason?"

"I decided to stay in and wash my hair."

"Wash your hair, that's not very nice, is it?" he asked. "Anyway, I will forgive you as it seems we're quits, so maybe arrange for another weekend if you want?"

"Maybe if you're lucky," she muttered.

Fletch walked away feeling well chuffed and more than anything, he had humiliated her in front of her mates and saved his own face. Now all he had to do his tell his mates.

He knew they had been watching the conversation so he walked over with an air of confidence.

"Morning boys, how's it going?" Fletch said with a big smile on his face.

"How did it go last night?" asked Jono.

"I didn't turn up," replied Fletch. "My grandparents came around so I stayed in and I forgot to phone her and tell her I wasn't going. I've just been over to apologise and she understands." He left out all the other details.

"You stood Beverly Lewis up?" enquired Ginner. "You for real?"

"Yep, let her know whose boss from the start," he replied.

Everyone shrugged their shoulders but seemed to accept his side of the events. All except Budgie, who had seen Ryan standing outside the pizza place when he was on the 5.30 bus to see his Nan but kept quiet for two reasons: one, he knew his mate would be feeling embarrassed by being stood up and two, he might be able to use this little piece of information in the future.

The kids were either milling around the bus stop, or those with money were busy buying sweets or magazines in the newsagents. At certain times, those without money would go in looking for the opportunity to obtain sweets without paying.

Mr and Mrs Richardson were always two-handed in the morning and on return of the school bus, knowing that pilfering would take place otherwise. They had a feeling it took place even when they were there but not as bad.

The kids had a scheme going however and would take turns to distract them. One would request the sweets from the top shelf, while another got the attention of the other leaving the shelf near the corner vulnerable.

The school bus was due to pick up at 8.15 and if it got to 8.20, some of the older boys would start looking at their watches.

"Give it another 5 minutes," they would say, "and if it's not here by then, we're off." But invariably, two minutes later, it would turn the corner and a few groans would go up.

The seating arrangement on the bus was a tradition cast in stone. The top deck was reserved for the older boys and a few selected girls. The sixth form occupied the rear seating. Next came the fifth-year lads, full of testosterone and as volatile as could be, trouble could kick off at any time and once a week it usually did. It was an intimidating place.

The fifth-year lads were ruled by the Riley twins, Sean and Steven, two of the nastiest pieces of work you could imagine. Their father gave them a regular good hiding and they in turn liked to do the same to others who crossed their paths or they just felt like picking on. They were part of an eight-man gang and if you fought one of them, you fought them all and everyone was fair game.

Budgie, Fletch, Jono and Ginner occupied the front seats and generally, the Riley twins left them alone as they knew Budgie could handle himself and he in turn looked after his mates.

The rest of the top deck was made up of a few fourth years and those unlucky enough to not get a seat on the lower deck. Robert Armstrong was in the fifth year, but he was the invisible type who no one really knew and no one really bothered about. He was as tall as those in his year but didn't stand up to his full height and he wore glasses that made him look geeky. He didn't knock around in the village after school, didn't stand out in classes as being a boff, and apart from Neil Thompson, who was of a very similar nature, he had no other friends. Robert preferred the comfort of his home with his doting mum and dad and his only passions were cars and working on Saturdays in his dad's car spares and accessories shop. He was always destined to work in the shop when he left school and eventually take it over, so he didn't need to stand out particularly academically and he certainly had no aspirations to be a sportsman.

The stairs to the school bus were halfway down, and Robert was sitting in the aisle seat in row three, reading his newly purchased car magazine. As Trenchy, one of the Riley twins' gang, passed by, he grabbed the magazine out of his hands and continued up the stairs to the top deck. Trenchy was a bully, the obnoxious type you wouldn't get tired of punching, but who always had the power of the Riley twins behind him.

Robert, instinctively and without thinking, rushed after whoever it was who had taken his magazine and ran up the stairs, an action he would regret for a long time to come. As he got behind the person holding his magazine, he got hold of his shoulder and pulled him around, demanding it back. He then suddenly realised whom he was pulling at and where he was, in the mouth of the tiger.

Trenchy turned around and hit Robert in the side of his face, sending him reeling backwards and onto an occupied seat. The occupier, not wanting to be associated with him, pushed Robert onto the floor. Trenchy pulled him up by his collar and tie and growled in his face, "What the hell do you think you're doing? Big mistake, twat, big mistake."

The mob were cheering as Robert descended the stairs, needless to say without the magazine.

Fletch was looking through the front window at Beverly Lewis, who was about to board the bus. He was deep in thought about how he would love to follow her up the stairs, getting a perfect view up her short skirt, when he heard the commotion.

"What's happening?" he asked.

"Armstrong is getting a good hiding off Trenchy," Ginner replied.

"Armstrong! What's he doing up here?" He turned his head towards the fracas.

"On a death wish, I think," said Budgie.

Armstrong made his way back to his seat trembling.

"What happened, mate?" asked Neil.

"Don't want to talk about it," he replied and he sat for the rest of the trip quiet and with his head down.

He managed to avoid bumping into Trenchy for the rest of the day and when school finished, Robert was hiding around the corner waiting for the Riley gang to push their way to the front and onto the school bus home. When it was clear, he ran across the playground and onto the bus. He sat in his usual seat next to Neil near the front on the lower deck. Today, however, he was grateful of the seats so he could make a quick getaway once they were home.

As the bus turned the corner into Hardwick, Trenchy came down the stairs and was waiting at the door of the bus. Robert saw this and hoped he had to be somewhere quick but his face drained as he got off the bus and saw Trenchy waiting for him. He tried to walk away but Trenchy was quickly on him.

"Right, you little shit, how dare you insult me in front of everyone on the bus this morning."

Robert tried to explain but was cut off by a fist in his face.

"If you want to keep your teeth in your mouth, you had better give me money every day from now on," Trenchy snarled. "And I mean every day, I want paying. Understand?"

Robert was the same height and weight as Trenchy but knew he wasn't up to fighting him, especially with all his mates around. He tried to pull away, but Trenchy held him tight. Everyone else watched and thought how bad it was, but no one wanted to speak up or do something about it because while they were picking on Armstrong, they weren't picking on them.

Trenchy then swanned over to his mates with a grin on his face like he had just threatened Henry Cooper.

"That little bastard's going to pay for what he did to me," he said.

Sean passed Trenchy what was left of his fag and they all wandered off.

Robert's life deteriorated from that day on.

As the weeks went by, he exhausted his savings and his wage for working Saturday and had reverted to stealing money from his mother's purse to fund the amount Trenchy was demanding. Despite paying him, Trenchy hit him on a regular basis to let him know he meant business.

He feigned illness as often as he dared to miss school. He had lost weight and wasn't sleeping and despite his parents seeing something was wrong and asking if they could help, he continued to bottle it all up inside. It came to a head when he was off school with a 'stomach ache' on the Monday unable to face school and Trenchy that day. He had taken money from the shop till on the Saturday and couldn't live with himself anymore. He was sitting in his bedroom facing his dad's whiskey bottle and a bottle of his mum's sleeping pills. A letter was at his side telling them how he had let them down and couldn't live with it anymore. He named Trenchy as the culprit in the hopes that he would be stopped from doing this to anyone else.

He poured a large glass of whiskey, which he had never tasted before, and the smell that came up from the glass made him question if he could actually go through and drink it all. He had thought of other methods, but this seemed the cleanest for his parents to find.

The full bottle of tablets was tipped onto the bed. He took a large handful and picked up the glass. He was about to swallow the tablets when he heard the back door open and his dad shouted up, "Robert I'm home, son, are you okay?"

He quickly scooped up the tablets and the whiskey and put them in his wardrobe. He walked downstairs holding his stomach.

"I've closed the shop for an hour," his dad said. "Come to see if you're all right and make you a sandwich."

His dad never shut up shop, he couldn't bear to think he might have missed a sale.

"I'm okay, Dad," he said. "Thanks for coming back."

"No problem, son," his dad replied. "You go and sit in the lounge and I'll bring you a sandwich and a nice cup of tea."

Robert walked into the lounge and from that moment, decided he wasn't going to end his life over a tosser like Trenchy. He would have to keep him sweet for the time being, but he was going to turn the tables on that bully. He started to plan T day, Trenchy day.

Chapter Five

It was Saturday evening in the first week of the school Easter holidays and Ryan was about to leave the house and join his mates.

"Right," he shouted to his mum and dad. "I'm off out, see you later."

"Hold on," shouted his dad. "I need to speak to you."

Ryan reluctantly went back into the living room. "What's up?"

His mum and dad were sat on the sofa with smug grins on their faces. "What're you doing next weekend?" his dad enquired.

"Same old, same old, I suppose, no football matches as it's Easter weekend, but we will find something to do."

"Well, me and your mum are going to your auntie's in Sunderland, fancy coming?"

"Do I have to?" replied Ryan. "I'd rather stay at home on my own, I am nearly 16 and you know I'll be fine."

"Well you can do that or..."

"Or what?" asked Ryan.

"Or we could drop you and your two mates off at the caravan on Friday and pick you up on our way back on Monday."

Ryan's mum and dad had a caravan on a campsite near Skegness. The site had a Cabaret club, football pitch, sports bar, beach and arcade. In other words, everything grown-ups, teenagers and kids wanted for a fun weekend. Ryan had been going since he was eight years old and over the years, had made friends with lads his own age there. He had taken Michael Johnstone and James Burgess on a few occasions over the years, but all three of them had never been at the same time and certainly never on their own.

"You serious?" asked Ryan.

"As long as you don't let us down," said Dad. "Keep it tidy and take your shoes off before you go in, and your mates."

"Of course, we will, thanks!" Ryan screamed as he left the room.

"Ryan!" his dad shouted.

"What?"

"You haven't said which of the two options you want."

"Are you havin' a laugh?" he replied. Ryan ran down to the shops wearing a smile from ear to ear. He found James and Jono sitting on the wall outside the shops. They were sat watching six twelve-year-old lads at the far end of the road, playing the rope trick, something that James and his mates had done when they were younger. There were three lads on one side of the road and three on the other. When a car came around the corner, they would all pull back. Pretending they were pulling an imaginary rope causing the driver to pull up quickly. It may have been funny to a twelve-year-old, but it was extremely dangerous. The best outcome for the lads would be if the driver pulled up and gave chase. They carried it out at the side of a narrow alleyway which lead into the estate, so they had a quick getaway.

A Ford Escort came around the corner at speed and the boys pulled back in unison. The driver hit his brakes and came to an emergency stop. The lads on the far side ran behind the car to join the others. With that, the four doors opened simultaneously and out got four burly twenty-odd-year-olds. The lads set off down the alley and the men gave chase.

"Bloody hell," said Jono. "If they catch them, they will kill them."

"You know as well as I do those lads will be away and into the estate and gone long before they get there," replied James.

With that, Ryan stopped in front of them almost out of breath. "Right, you pair, what you up to over Easter weekend?"

"I thought I might phone Debbie Harry up and see if she fancied a weekend in the Bahamas," Jono sarcastically replied.

"I might double date you with Kim Basinger," added Budgie.

"Well, you get yourselves off then and I'll ask Ginger and Lomas if they fancy joining me for four days at our caravan in Skegness without my parents," replied Ryan.

"Eh? You kidding?" Budgie asked.

"Nope, they're dropping me off Friday and picking up on Monday and everything in between is up for grabs, but don't worry, you fly off with your birds for the weekend, I wish you both luck."

"Hold on," said Jono. "If I really had the choice between the Bahamas and Skeggy, then I might consider letting Debbie down. I was thinking it's a bit far anyway for only four days anyway."

"Well, make your mind up quickly, boys, because you won't get a second chance."

"Okay, Skeggy it is," said Jono.

"Me too," said Budgie. "Kim will have to wait. My mates come first. I can't believe it how did you swing that one?"

"It was their suggestion," replied Ryan. "I can't believe it either, we've got three nights of partying to do, birds to shag, fun to have and I can't wait."

"How much cash do you think we'll need?" asked Jono.

"I don't know, depends how much beer we can drink and how many Jonny's we need to buy."

"I'm buying a large pack." Laughed Budgie.

"Yes," said Ryan. "A large one in number—you don't need a large one in size!"

The rest of the evening, they talked about the forthcoming holiday. James offered to take a few tins of toast toppers, Jono would take bread and milk and Ryan, cheese and butter. The beers would have to wait until they got there.

James arrived home to find Alex and his mum and dad glued to an episode of 'Rising Damp'.

Rigsby had been given a piece of wood by Phillip who had convinced him the wood was from an old tree in Africa and that if he got it smoking, it was guaranteed to make Miss Jones finally fall for his charms. His dad and Alex burst out laughing when Miss Jones poured water over the wood to get rid of the annoying smoke and Philip revealed it had actually fallen off the wardrobe.

"Right," said James. "Now I've got your attention, I've been invited to the caravan with Ryan for the weekend."

"That's kind of Ryan's mum and dad to take you," she said. "You make sure you're clean and tidy and help his mum clear up."

James was about to reveal that they weren't actually going to be there but decided against it, not that they would have said he couldn't go, but he would just get a list of dos and don'ts and have to phone home twice a day to let them know he was still alive.

"You're kidding," said Peter. "I wanted you to give me a hand this weekend, I'm doing a patio for someone."

"Peter," said Sheila sternly. "We haven't been able to take these lads away for two years so he isn't going to help do a patio, he is going to Skegness."

Peter knew when Sheila put the 'R' on the end of 'Pete' he was on a loser.

"Looks like you're doing your first foreigner this weekend, Alex," Pete said.

"Do I get paid?" he asked.

"Yep, if you do what I say and work hard I'll give you two pounds."

"Two pounds," shouted Alex. "For that, I'll work my bollocks off!"

"Alex!" shouted his mum. "Less of the bad language."

"Sorry, Mum," responded Alex, "but two quid, I can't believe it."

"I remember my first holiday with the lads," Peter said. "We went on the train all the way to Rhyl, had to change at Crewe. It was so far to us it was like going abroad. Well, it was abroad to us because it was in a different country, it was North Wales.

"I can distinctly remember two things," he said.

Everyone listened but knew there was one of his tall stories coming.

"I ran out of money after a couple of days and back then people didn't have phones in the house so I had to send a telegram home to ask them to wire me some money. The trouble was you had to pay so much per letter, so I kept it brief."

Alex fell for it. "What did it say, Dad?"

"It said, 'Dear mum, no fun, no mun, your son'."

"Did they send any?"

"Well, I went back to the post office next day to see, but there was a telegram waiting for me. It said, 'Dear lad, so sad, too bad, your dad'." He burst into laughter and repeated, "So sad, too bad, your dad."

To try and stop him laughing at his own jokes, Sheila asked, "What's the second thing you remember?"

"Well, it was long before your time, my sweet, but I met this girl from Prestatyn, not far from Rhyl, and after a couple of nights together, she kept saying to me, 'Oh Peter press tat in'." Laughing, "Oh press tat in," he repeated.

"I don't get it," said Alex. "I'm going to bed."

"I bet she didn't either," said Sheila.

Peter stopped laughing and just scowled at Sheila.

Once he had left the room, James said, "You've never given me you've never given me two pounds for a day's work, Dad."

"My words were two pounds, not two quid and that doesn't necessarily mean money, son. Read the small print, it could be two pounds of sand."

James laughed once it had clicked.

"You better not have him mixing cement and carrying slabs for a bag of sand, Pete," said Sheila.

Peter didn't respond. Columbo was about to start and it was one of the few Saturday nights they weren't going out.

Chapter Six

The next few days few days consisted of football on the rec, games of cards as the lads loved nothing better than a game of crib or shoot which involved three cards each, the banker turned his card over and you bet on whether you think you a have card in your three of the same suit that is higher. Trouble was you could lose a lot of money at the game so they had betting limits on to prevent any fallouts. There was also a lot of and talking about the forthcoming holiday which Ginge, lemmy and Banksy found extremely tedious.

It was Thursday night and next day they were off on holiday so James came in for his tea with the intention of staying in the night and packing so he was all ready for the morning.

His dad arrived home from work at the same time and was told by Sheila his tea was ready so to have it while it was hot and before he went upstairs and got changed.

Alex was already sat at the table and unusually Nev was home early as he was going to the cinema with Karen and was also sat waiting for his tea.

Sheila came into the room with a large tray of shepherd's pie courtesy of the school kitchen and put it in the centre of the table, the chips, veg and gravy were already there.

She served up a plate full for Peter, out it on a tray and then put the tray on his lap.

One by one, she served up the remainder of the food and for once they all complimented the school chef on a tasty pie.

The talk around the table was of James holiday in the morning and James still didn't confess to them being on there own although he had confided in Nev who also agreed it would be better not to let on until his return.

Sheila took the tray from Peters lap and together and swapped it with a bowl of treacle pudding.

Alex looked over to his father. His tie which he had only had to wear for the past few months since his promotion followed his profile down from his neck over his chest then protruded out and over his bursting stomach, it was a strange sight.

With sincerity in his voice, he commented on his dad's physique, "Dad, you need to go on a diet cos I am really worried."

"Don't be worried about me, son, I'm fine."

Nev, James and Sheila all stopped eating and looked across, Nev agreed. "He's right, Dad, you need to lose some weight for your health's sake."

"Listen, thank you for your concern but the summer is coming and I will be doing manual work of a weekend and I will be back to normal in no time."

"It's not your health I'm worried about," said Alex.

"Well, what is it then?"

"My worry is if you are sat in a meeting opposite people and one of your shirt buttons pops off, it could have some poor buggers' eye out!"

Fortunately, they had all stopped eating otherwise they would either have choked or there would have been treacle pudding and custard spat all over the dining table, they all burst out laughing.

Peter bit on his lip for two seconds then put his spoon in the bowl, the bowl on the floor then he burst out laughing too, it was a wonder a button didn't pop off.

He pointed at Alex. "One day, son, I swear to God, one day."

No one could finish their puddings for laughing and Alex was congratulated by everyone including his dad for the joke.

James finished packing, watched a bit of TV and then went to bed for an early night wanting to be fresh in the morning.

Chapter Seven

Friday morning finally came and James woke early and thought of the long weekend ahead, listening to Alex snoring. There was a light knock on the door and Nev popped his head around.

"Have a good time, mate," he said as he tossed two-pound coins onto his bed. "Have a drink on me."

"Oh, cheers, Nev," responded James. "You're a star."

"And another thing, no snogging any ugly birds," Nev smiled and was gone.

James decided he couldn't lie there anymore. He went to the bathroom, washed and dressed in jeans and a tee shirt and went down to the kitchen to find his mum just serving up beans on toast.

"Here you are, son, sit down and have a decent breakfast before you leave."

"Mum, can I take those tins of toast toppers?" enquired James.

"Yes, of course," she replied. "I'll give you a loaf as well?"

"No need," said James. "Jono is going to take a loaf."

Sheila looked at him inquisitively but never responded. His mum had been doing the ironing and James spied the black Fred Perry with the yellow motif that belonged to Nev, a shirt he had only worn once. James loved it; he was determined to buy the same one when he had enough money. Whilst Nev was three years older than James, he was big for his age and they were not far off a similar size. He finished his breakfast and as he left the room, he slipped the shirt from the pile and went upstairs. Alex was awake and saw the shirt in his hands as James came into the room.

"Has our Nev lent you his Fred Perry?" he asked.

"Well, sort of," replied James.

"What do you mean sort of?"

"Well, he didn't say I couldn't."

"Did you ask him?" asked Alex.

"Technically no, but he did tell me to have a good time. I'm sure he won't miss it until Monday."

"Wouldn't like to be you if he finds out," said Alex as he jumped out of bed.

James said his goodbyes to Alex, picked up his case and his wallet and left the room.

"James!" came the shout from his dad's room.

James walked into the bedroom to see his dad propped up in bed.

"Have a good time son, you got enough money?"

"Not sure, Dad," he replied.

Peter opened his side table and extracted three one-pound coins. "Here, I'm sure you can make use of these."

"Oh thanks," he said. "Really appreciate that."

"Don't tell your mum," his dad said. "She thinks I'm skint."

"Your secret's safe with me," replied James.

There was a ring at the doorbell and James went downstairs. His mum had opened the door to find Ryan stood there and his mum and dad sitting in the car. She waved to them a mouthed "thanks for taking him." The Fletchers waved back smiling.

James kissed his mum on the cheek.

"Here you are, son," she said, "a bag with toast toppers, a tin of corned beef and some biscuits and a couple of quid for you. Don't tell your dad, he thinks you should earn everything you get. We can't expect Mr and Mrs Johnstone to provide all your food as well as take you away for the weekend."

"I won't tell Dad, Mum," said James with a smile on his face. "See you Monday!"

"Oh, and make sure you buy a big box of chocolates for Mrs Fletcher," she shouted as he went down the path.

The seven pounds he had accumulated this morning together with the ten he had saved from his 50p a week pocket money and working with his dad at weekends meant he was going to have the best holiday ever.

They called at Michael Johnston's house next, he had packed the previous night so he would be ready for the early start.

Pride of place in his case was a brand-new pair of Rupert bear check trousers and black braces which he was going to surprise his mates with on Saturday night.

He had been to town the previous Saturday and when passing a men's shop it had a mannequin dressed in the trousers with a tee shirt and braces.

He was the quiet one of the three and wouldn't normally wear such loud clothing but he had a rush of blood to the head and could resist trying them on.

The young sale assistant convinced him he looked smart and the girls wouldn't be able to resist him and in the end, he gave in and bought the trousers and the braces.

Jono had a dry sense of humour, an athletic body bordering on skinny which made his nose look bigger than it actually was, hence the nickname, Bugle. He has hated the nickname at first but the more it was said the more he tried to not let it show everyone it upset him.

Even so, he wore his hair long which softened his features.

He was an exceptional footballer and several scouts had had him on their radar for the last year, it was inevitable he would make it professionally at some level.

Michael came out of the house with a case in one hand and a carrier bag full of goodies in the other. Jono's sister, Megan, followed him down the path. She was two years younger and had a massive crush on Budgie. She wouldn't have normally been up at this time on a weekend, but she couldn't resist the chance for a peak at Budgie through the car window and she had been up for an hour making herself presentable. She gave him a big smile and a wave as the car pulled away and wished she were going with him.

They arrived at the site two hours later. During the journey, Mrs Fletcher had read them a set of rules and dos and don'ts to which all three unanimously agreed. They would have agreed to running around the site naked at that point to make sure the holiday went through. James told them the story about Alex and his dad's shirt button popping off which they all found hilarious.

Mr Fletcher opened up the caravan while the lads got the luggage and goodies out.

Mr and Mrs Fletcher made up the two beds and instructed the lads to strip them on Monday so the sheets could be taken home to be washed.

They looked around the van. "Are you sure you'll be okay?" asked Mrs Fletcher.

"Mum, we will be now please just go we will be fine," replied Ryan.

They said their good byes and drove away.

As soon as they were out of sight, the three lads jumped in the air together and slapped hands.

"Right, let's party," shouted Ryan.

"Lock up your daughters," responded Jono.

"Unless you guys have any other ideas, let's unpack, have a sarnie and walk down to the club and see what's going on over the weekend."

"Sounds good to me, Ryan, old pal," responded Jono.

Ryan's mum had packed enough food to feed a small country, so they pooled the three goody bags and decided on cheese and tomato sandwiches and crisps followed by chocolate digestives and a cup of tea. Jono was in charge of buttering bread, Ryan putting on the cheese and tomato and Budgie making the tea.

Easter was early in the year and being by the coast it was a degree or two colder than home, but it was partly cloudy with patches of blue sky.

"At least it's not raining," said Budgie.

"I couldn't care less if it does," said Jono. "I'm going to enjoy myself come rain or shine."

They arrived at the main entertainment area where the cabaret club, arcade, bowling green and football pitch was. This is where most teenagers congregated. Ryan looked around for anyone he knew, but saw no one. As they passed the club, there was a notice board outside showing tonight's entertainment: a band called Tina and the Touch of Gold.

"My god," said Fletch. "I spent the best hour of my life last year looking up Tina's short skirt. We had the front table and I'm not kidding I could see her black knickers and I'm sure her fanny was winking at me."

"Dream on, Fletch lad, dream on," said Jono.

"Honestly," he carried on. "She is a babe, long brown hair, I dreamt about her for weeks after."

"Adult's football match Sunday morning," said James. "We're on for that."

"Look," said Jono. "A deep-sea fishing trip tomorrow, fancy it?" he asked.

The board was advertising a five-hour fishing trip off the coast of Skegness for two pounds including transfers.

"Only been fishing once," replied Budgie. "Went with our Nev to some lake, most boring day of my life and all I caught was a cold."

"I fancy it," said Fletch.

"Come on, Budge, it will be a laugh," pleaded Jono.

"Go on then," he replied.

They walked to the kiosk where you booked day trips and found an attractive young lady sitting behind a desk.

"We're interested in the deep-sea fishing," enquired Jono.

"You look like proper seafaring lads," she responded. "I bet you've landed a few in your time," she added with a smile.

"We can pull 'em out without even throwing in any bait," responded Ryan. "I bet you would be hooked if you came with us."

She laughed. "Sorry lads, I've got a boyfriend, but nice try. Tell you what, the boat takes eight fishermen and I only have three booked on. I was afraid I might have to cancel it so I will do you a deal: three for a fiver."

"Deal," said Jono keenly.

After they had paid the money, the girl gave them their instructions. "Right don't be late, be at the entrance to the site at 8.00 am, take a warm jacket. Once you get to the harbour, check in with the captain. You will have time for some breakfast before it sets off at 9.30, but take my advice and don't eat too much. The boat returns at 1.30 and you should be back here for 2.15. Everything clear?"

"Crystal," replied Fletch. "I'll catch us a cod and we can share that with a bag of chips."

"I don't think there are many cod swimming off the coast of Skegness," she replied. "But I admire your enthusiasm." She gave them the tickets and they left.

"I'm defo in there," said Fletch. "I'm going to win her over when I catch a furkin."

"What's a furkin?" asked Jono.

"A furkin big fish," replied Fletch.

"The only fish you might get will be battered from the chippy," said Budgie.

"Well, we'll see about that, 20p to the one who catches the most?"

"You're on," they both replied.

"I wonder why she said don't eat too much?" asked James.

"She's probably never even been on a boat so what does she know," replied Fletch.

They walked into the arcade and surveyed the clientele. Two girls both quite attractive stood out amongst the rest.

"Two nice looking females, two o' clock," said Fletch.

The other two turned their heads in that direction.

"Mmmmmm baggy blondie," said Jono.

"I don't mind the other to be honest," replied Budgie.

"Hold on, I saw them first. Wow, forget them—look at their mate just walking over," said Fletch. He watched as a girl with long black hair, a short skirt and a short sheepskin jacket joined them. "I'll have her. I don't believe our luck, three nice birds together, let's take a walk over."

They were stood by one of the machines trying to look like cool.

"Hello, girls," said Fletch. "Had any luck on the machines?"

"Yes," said the blonde. "I just won the jackpot, two weeks for two in the Seychelles, fancy joining me?"

"Providing it's after the football season," said Fletch. "We're footballers so we can't go away before mid-May."

"Is that right?" asked the blonde. "Well, why aren't you playing this weekend?"

"Gaffer gave us the weekend off, we play for Sheffield Wednesday reserves and they haven't got a game," said Jono.

"You could have come up with something a bit more original like astronauts or nuclear scientists," said the one with black hair.

"It's true, are you saying we don't look like footballers?"

"Yes of course you do, providing you're playing Subbuteo," responded the blonde.

"You're quite funny for a girl," said Fletch. "What do you three do anyway?"

"We're all models," said the blonde.

"What do you model? Knickers and bras for little woods catalogue?" James enquired hopefully. "I've spent hours looking at them pages of me mum's catalogue."

"Yes, I have seen that catalogue and most of the pages are stuck together," said Jono who immediately regretted, it thinking it was a bit course.

"That's all you fellas think of. No, we are catwalk models."

"Yeah, yeah, yeah, how come you're in Skegness and not France then?" asked Jono.

"Our agent gave us the weekend off."

They finally established that the blonde one was called Becky, long black hair was called Clare and the third Joanne. They were staying in Becky's parents' caravan, which had a toilet and bathroom so they must have been posh. They lived in Leeds and were all fifteen years old, nearly sixteen. Similar to the lads except that they said they were sixteen almost seventeen.

Fletch informed them they had their own caravan which they had bought together with their first month's wages. The girls took it all with a pinch of salt but went along with it.

"Shall we have a walk to the beach?" asked Fletch.

"Can do," responded Becky. "But don't count on us flattening any sand hills."

"You should be so lucky," said James.

After an hour's walk on the beach, they arranged to meet in the club later that night. The girls would have no trouble getting in, as they would be with their parents. The lads would have to bluff their way in. A natural pair up between Fletch and Becky, Jono and Jo and James and Clare seemed to be how it was going to pan out, but not cast in stone.

For the rest of the afternoon, they took a football onto the grassed area near their caravan and it didn't take long before another six lads had arrived and asked if they could join in and not much longer before they had jumpers for goal posts and a six a side.

Afterwards, the lads took their towels and toiletries and walked across to the shower block. The caravan didn't have the luxury of those facilities. There were three showers and all three were taken when they arrived. They stood patiently and eventually, two became available. Fletch and James grabbed one each.

Eventually, Jono got in the third shower. The water was like ice for the first two minutes until warm water gradually came through.

"Are you in yet, Jono?" asked Fletch.

"Not yet, the waters too cold," he replied.

"You in Budge?"

"I'm in, and it's better in than out."

"I'm in too and it's defo better in than out."

"Ooh I'm in now," said Jono, "and you're right it's better in than it was out."

After hearing the exchanges between cubicles for five minutes, a man waiting to go in had finally had enough, he banged on the cubicle door James was in and in the deepest, gruffest voice shouted, "If you don't hurry up and get out of them showers, I will be in and throw you all out!"

James opened his door and peeked out at the voice before he gave a response. He saw a six-foot six-inch shaved-headed monster glaring at him.

"Just getting out, mate," he said.

The other two heard James and realised the voice meant what he had said. They sheepishly left the cubicles and passed the man.

"Sorry, mate," Fletch said. "Didn't realise anyone was waiting."

The voice grunted and had to turn sideways to get into the cubicle.

"Phew," Jono said as they got outside. "He was like a brick shit house."

"I was going to give him some lip but luckily I thought I would check him out first," replied James.

They got back to the van and made themselves corned beef hash and beans topped with loads of brown sauce of which they were extremely proud.

"Pity we haven't got a camera to take a picture of our creation before we eat it," said Fletch.

"Our mums won't believe it," replied James. "It's almost too good to eat."

After they devoured the meal, they washed up, just in case the girls came back, changed and were ready for the night's festivities. James had showed off the black Fred Perry to his mates but declared he was saving that shirt for Saturday night.

He wore a pair of shiny blue stay press trousers and a white Ben Sherman, a hand me down from Nev.

Fletch wore his 22-inch bell bottom jeans and a white tee shirt and Jono kept his Rubert bear trousers under wraps and wore flared trousers and a maroon grandad shirt.

They all looked in the mirror and admired what they saw. "Phew, a sight for sore eyes boys, them girls won't be able to keep their hands off us," said Jono.

"Right," said Fletch as they walked to club. "If you're not eighteen, you have to be with your parents so we've got two options: try and pass for eighteen, but if the bouncers don't buy it, we're screwed, or try and bunk in with some adults as though we are with them."

"Let's go with the second option," said Jono, who was the youngest looking of the three.

As they arrived at the club, they saw two bouncers checking the adults as they walked up for their membership cards.

James took charge. "Right, Jono, see the couple coming around the corner? Go up and ask them the time before they get to the door, loads of smiles and chit chat and keep walking at the side of them until you are inside, avoid eye contact with the bouncers."

Jono carried out the procedure perfectly. Two minutes later and two couples were approaching, so Fletch did the same thing. Fletch performed perfectly, nestled nicely between the two ladies like he was one of their sons.

James could probably have passed for eighteen but decided not to risk it, he then saw the voice coming around the corner.

"Hey up, mate," said James as he walked at the side of the man and his wife. "Sorry about before."

"No problem, mate, but you were getting on my nerves with all that, who's in and whose out shite."

The couple nodded to the bouncers who they obviously knew and the bouncers, seeing James talking to them, never gave him a second look. They were past the bouncers and through the doors.

"See you later," said James as he breezed over to his two mates.

"Bloody hell, you came in with him?" asked Jono.

"Yes, I was just telling him if he knocked on my shower door that loud again the next shower he took would be in the hospital."

Fletch laughed. "The next one you take might be in fantasy island!"

"Anyway, boys, we're up and running, let's get a table in the corner at the back, we don't want anyone questioning us. Get that one over there and I'll get the drinks."

The club was huge, holding about seven hundred people, and the bar was about fifty yards long with beer pumps every few yards. James and Jono got the table and scoured the room to see if the girls were in. Fletch came back with three cokes and two pints of beer on a tray.

"How did you get them?" asked James.

Fletch looked back at the bar. "See that fella with the blue shirt on, well he took a load of drinks back to his table and the barman then put two more pints on the bar for him. The other barman then brought my change and walked off, so when the guy serving him turned to pull some shorts, I took the pints and shot off."

The man with the blue shirt could be seen demonstrating to the barman. Fletch sat down quick with his back to the bar in case he was rumbled. They each had a coke in front of them and the beers in the middle, they could always say they weren't theirs if someone asked.

The DJ announced Tina and the Touch of Gold and on stage they came, Tina wearing short black skirt, white shirt, black boots and black tights.

She was everything Fletch had described her and more. The three lads looked on with mouths wide open. James finally snapped out of it and saw the three girls with four adults. They had a table but were trying to get more chairs. James stood up and caught the attention of Becky. They had spare chairs at their table, so he gestured to her and her mates to sit with them. She looked over and acknowledged his suggestion and had a word with her dad.

They all looked over at the boys table and her dad said a few more words before the girls picked up their bags and walked towards them.

"Hiya, boys," Jo said. "You looking for a good time?"

"We most certainly are," said Jono, pulling out the chairs for each of them.

"What would you like to drink?" asked Fletch.

"We will get our own, thanks," said Becky. "But do me a favour, put them beers on the table at the side. My dad will go mad if he sees we're with boys drinking beer. Anyways, what're footballers doing drinking beer?" she asked.

"Listen when you're as fit as us a few beers doesn't make any difference," replied James.

"How did you three get in anyway? Without an adult?" asked Clare.

"We're celebrities around here," replied James. "The bouncers know us and welcome us in with open arms."

The three girls smiled and didn't respond. At first, they had sat three and three but after a few dances, they paired up as they had in the afternoon and sat in couples with Fletch the first to brave it and get hold of Becky's hand. The night went well and they danced away to Tina and the Touch of Gold.

The girls went off to the toilets as did Fletch who on his return, possessed one full pint and one three-quarter full pint.

"Where did you get them from?" asked Jono.

"Passed a table and someone must have left them."

James tracked his route back and saw two couples who must have been for a dance and the men looking around to see which waitress had taken their glasses. They all got their heads down and were pleased to see the girls come back to give them some camouflage. The night went well, Fletch managed another few beers by one means or another and they were gutted when Becky's dad came over to announce they were calling it a day.

"Would it be all right if we stayed a bit longer?" asked Becky.

"No, come on girls it's 11.00 pm."

"We need to be out early in the morning on the fishing trip so we need to go," said Fletch hoping to impress her dad.

The three girls thanked the lads for a nice night and promised to see them the same place at the same time tomorrow night.

The lads got back to the van with a few wobbles on the way, and decided they were starving and tomato soup and bread seemed the easy option. They left the washing, thinking it could stay until a more suitable time. Fletch set the clock for 7.20 am and they went to bed. The sleeping arrangements were Fletch in the double bedroom as it was his caravan. Jono and James in the pull-down double bed. They could have separated with one of them sleeping on one of the side sofas, but that would have meant making it up each night and clearing it away in the morning so it was easier to sleep in the one bed and just push it back up in the morning.

They laid in bed in the pitch black but for an orange glow from a streetlight that seeped through a chink in the curtains and James shouted, "Are you having a toss, Fletch?"

"No," replied Fletch.

"You are, I can hear you!"

"I'm not, trust me."

"I thought I heard you as well," said Jono.

"I'm not," Fletch insisted, "I was rubbing my nose."

"Oh that old chestnut," said Budgie.

"I got caught having one a couple of weeks ago," said Jono.

James turned towards him. "You're kidding, who caught you?" he asked.

"My dad, I was just getting to the point of no return, my eyes were rolling back when I got the biggest crack on the back of my head, I couldn't believe it, I nearly shit myself."

"Don't tell lies, are you serious, what did he say?" Fletch shouted over from his bedroom.

"It's true, honest, he said, 'You dirty little bleeder'."

"I said, 'Dad, I'm nearly sixteen, it's only natural'. He said, 'maybe, but you shouldn't be doing it when we are all sat around the dinner table!'"

Fletch and Budgie had been taken in big time and burst out laughing.

"You got me there, pal," said Budgie.

"Me too, you wanker," said Fletch.

This brought another laugh from the three of them and after a long day, the effects of the alcohol they were all asleep in minutes.

Chapter Eight

The alarm woke them bang on at 7.20 am.

"Come on, lads," shouted James. "Let's get dressed."

"I'm just going to take 50p for a breakfast," said Fletch. "Everything is paid for and we will be back at two-ish so we won't need anymore and we might lose it or the notes will get wet on the boat."

"Good idea," said James. "We'll all do the same."

They all dressed in jeans, jumpers and remembered the advice and took a coat each.

They locked up the caravan and James was put in charge of the keys.

They got to the gates to find three middle-aged men all with their own rods and tackle.

"Morning, you lot look professionals," Fletch said.

"You lot look rough," replied one of the men. "Did you have your first pint last night?"

"We could drink you fellas under the table," Jono replied. "We are eight-pints-a-night lads us."

The three men laughed. "What, eight pints of milk?" one responded.

With that, a mini-bus pulled up and they all got on.

"Okay fellas," said the driver. "It will take us thirty minutes to get to the harbour so relax."

The lads took the opportunity to catch up on their sleep.

No one spoke for the rest of the journey and eventually, they pulled up into the car park.

The driver pointed over the harbour wall down to the fishing boats lined up, side by side. "See that one with the green flag and the man sat at the back? That's your boat and Captain Saunders. Go and check in with him and then come back up here. If you want a breakfast, I would recommend the café over the road, Lily's, see it?"

The boat will be back for around 1.45pm and I will be here to pick you up.

The boys said thanks, the three men said they had already eaten and started down to the harbour. They arrived at the boat and the first thing that struck the lads was how small it was.

"Bit small for nine of us, isn't it, mate?" said Fletch.

"First of all, I'm your captain not your mate and second, the QE2 got delayed in the Caribbean so you'll have to put up with this today."

He had a voice that sounded like he had been gargling with gravel for a month.

"You three bring your tackle aboard and we will get set up. You lads go and find something to do for an hour and I will set your rods up. Be back here 9.25 sharp he growled and if your late don't come here and say sorry because it is you who will be late and so us that will be sorry."

The lads nodded and made their way to the café. "Miserable old sod, I say we're late on purpose just so we can say we are late and we hope you're sorry," said Fletch.

"We better not he has our money and he's the type to set off without us," replied James.

They entered the café and saw only three spare seats at a table already occupied by someone behind a newspaper who had a full mug of tea and a smouldering cigarette in an ashtray in front of him.

They walked over and sat down; the paper never moved.

Jono gave the table a nudge with the palm of his hand, spilling tea into the saucer. No reaction from behind the paper. Again, he nudged the table spilling more tea, again no reaction.

Fletch poked his head over the newspaper to find an old tramp type man fast asleep. "He's out for the count," said Fletch as a round woman wearing an apron that looked like it needed a good wash came up.

"What can I get you boys?" she asked.

"Can we get a full English and a cup of tea for 50p each?" asked James.

"It's actually 60p but I will knock off a sausage each and call it 50p."

"Thanks," said James.

"Not sure I can stomach a full English," said Jono. "Feel a bit rough after last night."

"Me too," said Fletch.

"Shut up, you tarts," said James. "You need something in your stomach before you go out for the morning."

"True but that bird at the kiosk said don't eat a lot," said Jono.

She's probably never seen a fishing boat so what does she know replied Fletch.

They both reluctantly agreed. They ate the breakfast and felt a little better and called the round lady over for the bill. The man behind the paper had not moved the whole time.

Just as they were about to leave, Fletch said, "You walk out, I won't be a minute." He got out his Harley Davison lighter he carried everywhere with him. Michael and James headed for the door as Fletch lit the newspaper halfway up and then made for the door. Outside, they peered through the window to see Fletch bent over in front of the newspaper and then the man jump up trying to let go of the newspaper that was in flames.

"Run," said Fletch as he came out of the café. They ran as fast as they could around corner.

"Are you for real?" asked James out of breath. "You could have killed him."

"I thought it was hilarious," said Fletch. "Imagine when he woke up seeing the paper on fire, he will think it was the cigarette that started it."

"I can't believe you did that," said James. "It was funny, but I just hope he's all right."

"At least I lit it halfway up, imagine if it had been from the bottom," replied Fletch.

They got to the boat at 9.25 exactly, still talking and laughing about the paper going up in flames.

"Aye, aye, Captain," said Jono. "Bang on time, three land lubbers reporting for duty. I hope its ship shape and Bristol fashion." He put his hand up to his forehead in salute.

"Comedian are we, lad?" asked the captain. "You been at sea before, have you?"

"Don't worry about me, Captain. Hard as nails, me," he said, "got sea faring blood flowing in my veins."

The captain smiled, revealing several missing teeth. "That's good," he said. "'Cos we've a slight swell out there today. Come on, then. Let's get going and see how big and tuff you lads are"

"By the way," he barked. "Once we are out there, we ain't coming back for three hours so be prepared."

The three lads looked at each other and shrugged their shoulders. The boat set off and the lads sat at the back. "Don't see what he's going on about," said Jono. "The sea is as flat as a pancake."

After five minutes, they passed the harbour entrance and hit a slight wave and a breeze in their face, as they turned left. After another minute, the boat was bouncing up and down as it hit against the swell.

Three minutes later, Jono went green.

They eventually stopped and anchored up but the bobbing up and down on the sea quickly affected Jono. He moved to the side of the boat and threw up. The problem was it was wind side and the sick came back and pebble dashed both him and Fletch. This caused Fletch to have the same reaction but fortunately, he chucked it over the opposite side. Jono joined him and within three minutes, they had both lost their breakfast and more.

The captain came over to them, "Fancy a nice bowl of liver and onions?" he asked.

The two brought more up from where they didn't know.

"Do worry, only another two and a half hours to go," he added.

The two just wanted to die. "Throw me overboard and leave me to drown," muttered Jono as sick dripped off his chin.

Fletch fell into the bottom of the boat and just sat there. James, meanwhile, was pulling in his first catch. The captain came over and gave him instructions and after what seemed an age, a large whiting landed on the floor of the boat. The captain took the hook from its mouth and threw it in a bucket.

After an hour, it was James-three and the three expert fishermen-one.

"Must be beginner's luck," shouted James.

The boat continued to bob up and down and just when Fletch and Jono thought there was no more sick left in their stomachs, a load more would come up. Their stomachs, throats and heads hurt like they had never hurt before. The nausea and swooning heads were an experience they never wanted to repeat.

Eventually, the captain ordered them to reel in their lines, as it was time for home. It finished at James-four and the three experts-three. James felt like he had won top goal scorer for the season.

As the boat made its way home, Ryan was laying on his back groaning and Jono was at the side of him on his side curled up in a ball and fast asleep, bits of sick were floating in water which went from the front to the back of the boat as it bobbed up and down occasionally washing against the lads.

Opposite them was James and the three men with the captain at the wheel in the front who turned around and growled, so much for being hard as nails.

The three men looked down and laughed and then one got up and took out the biggest fish that had been caught out of the bucket.

He looked at it and said, "Boy, do you smell and you is ugly."

It had big lips a wide-open mouth and bulbous eyes. He put it on the deck of the boat an inch from Jono's nose.

He sat back down and they all watched. After a minute, a nostril twitched and 30 seconds later, it twitched again. It then twitched six times in quick succession and then Jono who must have been having a nightmare about boats and fish gradually opened his eyes which took 15 seconds to focus on the face of the fish staring right at him.

As if a bolt of lightning had gone through his body from the waist up, he shot up vertically and then gradually lay back down.

James and the three men burst out laughing.

Jono uttered the word, bastards then with great pain he turned over away from the fish.

Not much sea faring blood flowing through them veins either added the captain.

Jono tried to lift his arm and stick two fingers up but he didn't have the energy to part his two fingers.

They eventually arrived back on port and a man on the key side threw captain the ropes and he tied her up.

As the three men were getting off James asked, "Aren't you taking the fish you caught?"

"No, you keep them lad," one replied. "See you at the bus."

James didn't have a clue what he was going to do with them, but he tied them to a piece of rope the captain gave him and got off the boat. Jono and Fletch couldn't move.

"Come on, lads," growled the captain. "I got another trip in an hour."

He helped them to their feet, but they needed the captain on the boat and James on the dock to get them onto the quayside safely.

"I need to lie down," said Jono.

"You've been doing that for three hours," said James.

"Me too," said Fletch. "Let's get on that bench over there and come around for ten minutes, I don't feel well."

They staggered over to the bench and flopped down. James tied the fish to the side of the bench and sat down, too.

Fifteen minutes later, James woke. "Shit," he said. "What time is it?"

Jono woke and wearily looked at his watch. "Quarter to two."

"Shit," James said again. "The bus."

He jumped up and ran to the top of the road and looked across at the car park, where he saw no mini-bus. He walked across. There were coaches and cars everywhere, but no minibus. "Bastard," he muttered to himself. He walked back down to the harbour to find the two lads fast asleep.

"Come on," he said. "The bloody bus has left without us."

Fletch stirred. "You kidding? The three fellas knew we were down here."

"I know they had the gob on 'cos I caught more fish than them, I think."

"Bastards," said Jono as he pulled himself up. "What do we do now? We've got no money for bus fares and it's too far to walk."

James looked at the fish. "I know but we have seven fish, they must be worth something. There's a coach party up there, let's see if anyone will buy them." James gave Fletch the fish. "I caught them and have sorted them out up to now so it's one of your turns to carry them."

"I don't think I could carry myself," said Jono. "Never mind some smelly fish."

Fletch got hold of the rope and was surprised how heavy they were. They walked to the top of the road to find a load of men on a day trip away at the seaside.

"Any of you fellas want to buy some fish?" asked James.

"Only if they come battered with chips," replied one of the men.

"Please, will you? We need money for a bus home as we've missed our lift."

"How much do you want for them?" one asked.

"25p each," replied James.

"Frigging hell," replied the man. "Where you going to, London?"

"No, Skegness, but we're starving as well, not had anything to eat for hours."

"I tell you what," he said. "I'll give you a pound for the lot."

"Are you pissed?" asked his mate. "What are you gonna do with seven fish?"

"Take them home and cook them," he said.

"Well, rather you than me," he replied. "And the bus driver is going to love you taking them smelly things on."

"Don't listen to him," said James. "We've got a deal."

Fletch handed the rope of seven fish and the man went in his pocket but only had 90p in change.

"Sorry, lad," he said. "It's that or nothing."

James reluctantly agreed and then took the money.

"Spot of luck there, James, well done and congratulations," said Jono.

"I know, I'm just a born fisherman, let's find out where the bus station is and the next bus home."

"I'm beginning to get hungry," said Fletch. "But not sure if I can stomach anything just yet."

"Well, we better find out how much the bus fare is before we buy anything. Come on," said James. "There's the station over there."

They walked across and established the next bus was in thirty minutes and three fares would cost 45p which left 45p for food. They went into a shop and decided upon a loaf of bread and three packets of crisps. They sat on the wall outside and made crisp sandwiches. Fletch put the sandwich to his mouth but quickly pushed it away.

"Bloody hell, my hands stink," he said.

"Mine too," agreed James. "But I'm too hungry to care."

They bit into the sandwiches but only ate half way in so they didn't get too close to their hands. They finished up and made their way to the bus stand.

"Whose idea was this fishing carry on?" asked Fletch.

"Not mine," said James. "But I'm pleased we came, shall we do it again tomorrow?"

"You can piss off," said Jono. "Not one of my better ideas."

They finally got back to the van and collapsed on the settees.

"If them fellas are in the club tonight," said James. "I'm going to crack one of them, they left us stranded on purpose."

"Me too," said Fletch. "Not a nice thing to do."

A combination of the traumatic morning and the sea air meant they fell fast asleep for nearly two hours.

Chapter Nine

Fletch was first to wake. "Bloody hell, lads it's nearly six o' clock. Come on, we need to make ourselves pretty for the girls tonight."

"Forget it then, we've only got an hour, so Jono's got no chance," replied James as he stretched out on the settee.

"Oh, thanks very much, John Travolta," said Jono.

"Come on boys, seriously, we need to smarten ourselves up, what're we going to do for tea?"

"Let's just get a burger or something from the café before we go into the club," replied Jono.

"Sounds good to me. Come let's get showered," said James.

They got their towels and made their way to the shower block. None of the showers was taken and they quickly undressed and got in one each. The banter started and who's in and who's out started again when the voice boomed out. "We're not going through that load of shit again, are we, lads?"

They didn't respond but said no more and were showered and out as quickly as they could.

"All right, mate," asked James as he got out. "We were as quick as we could be."

"Yes, I know, thanks," he said. "Listen I take it from last night's carry on that you three are here on your own and need someone to take you in the club."

"Yes, you're right," said Fletch. "My mum and dad's van but they aren't here, how did you know."

"Never mind, meet me outside the club at 7.30 and you can come in with me and my Mrs."

"Oh cheers," they all said at once. "You're a star."

As they got outside, Fletch turned to James. "Good job you didn't crack him after all, Budgie."

"You're right, mate, I might just have regretted it."

They got themselves ready and James put on his brother's Fred Perry.

"She won't be able to resist me in this," he said looking in the mirror.

"Smart, that, mate," replied Jono. "Dead smart."

"Fletch would you mind if I got changed in your room?" asked Jono.

"Why you getting shy now you've finally grown a few pubes," he replied.

"No let me, I just want to try my new clothes on in the room."

"Go on then, but don't mess it up, that bed might be seeing some action tonight," said Fletch.

"Only likely this room is likely to see is if you have another toss."

"I told you I was rubbing my nose."

"Yeah, yeah, yeah," he replied as he walked into the bedroom and closed the door.

Jono took his case in and unpacked his clothes. He put on his white Ben Sherman, then his Rupert bear trousers then spent five minutes trying to attach the braces to the tops of his trousers.

"What you doing you big tart," shouted Fletch, thinking he must be up to no good in his room.

"Nearly ready," came the reply.

Two minutes later, out came Jono. "Look and weep, suckers," he proudly said.

James and Fletch looked in amazement with mouths open and for 30 seconds couldn't speak, it was totally out of character for him.

Eventually, James said, "Jono, what the hell have you got on, you look like a pair of curtains."

"You want to pull yourself together," added Fletch.

The two lads burst out laughing.

"I'll tell you, mate, these trousers are the in thing and everyone in London is wearing braces."

"We're not in London, we are in Skeggy, and you look a right pillock," said Fletch, "they will bar me from the club if I'm seen with you in that gear."

"I don't care, and if me and my bird have to sit on our own then fine."

"She will run a mile when she sees you dressed like that," said James.

"Enough, get over it, you two wouldn't know fashion if it hit you in the face," said Jono feeling a bit less sure of himself.

They all splashed on enough hi karate aftershave to bath in and set off for the club. Sure enough, the voice came around the corner at 7.30 holding his wife's hand.

"These are the three lads I told you about," he said. "I'm lucky to still be here, I thought they were going to give me good hiding when they came out of the shower."

She laughed. "He looks a lot scarier than he actually is," his wife said. "He is a real softy really."

"What's your name?" asked Fletch.

"I'm Gus and this is Penny."

"Well I'm Ryan, this is James, and this is Michael."

"Nice shirt, James," Penny said.

"Oh thanks, it's my favourite."

"It's his brothers as well," said Jono.

"Cheers for that," replied James.

"You look very er, nice too," said Penny to Jono, "a bit loud but er nice," she added.

"Thanks," replied Jono, "these two think I look a right plonker but they haven't got style and I don't care."

Gus didn't know what to say so decided to say nothing apart from wear a grin and wink at James.

They all shook hands and walked up to the doors.

"All right, Gus, all right, Penny?" enquired one of the bouncers.

"We're great, thanks."

"These lads with you?" he asked.

"They are tonight," replied Gus.

"Good," said the bouncer. "It means they don't have to try and bunk in with random couples like last night."

The three lads all blushed at once. "Sorry, mate," said Ryan. "We have a van on here but my mum and dad aren't."

"Don't worry, I recognise you," replied the bouncer. "But behave please."

"We will," said James.

"But ay it's not fancy dress you know," he shouted to Jono.

Jono was about to turn around and tick two fingers up but decided against it, instead he turned around and said, "If it was you'd be okay you could come as the God father." The bouncer was wearing a black suit, dickie bow and had greased back hair and a moustache. James got hold of Jono and walked him briskly through the doors before the bouncer changed his mind.

"I suppose you're meeting them birds?" asked Penny.

"Hopefully." Grinned James. "They should be here soon."

"Right, you go and get your table and I will bring you over three halves of lager," said Gus.

"You sure?" asked James. "You don't need to do that, but thanks."

"Save you taking drinks off tables as you walk past." Laughed Penny.

For the second time that evening, the three blushed. The lads went and got a table and positioned six chairs around.

"Well, it just goes to show that you may think you're one step ahead of everyone else but you're not," said Jono.

"I can't believe we were rumbled coming in and getting the drinks," replied James.

Jono and Fletch went and got a table while James went to the café and got burger and chips three times and took them on a tray back to the table which took him a while to locate them.

After they finished, Fletch got the chewing gum out and passed it around. "We don't want burger breath when we are sticking our lips on the birds," he said.

Gus came over with three halves. "Bit of advice," he said. "Drink halves when you are underage but it doesn't look as obvious that you're drinking alcohol as when you have pints in front of you."

"Cheers, Gus, you're right," said Fletch. The other two thanked him as well.

"You playing football tomorrow?" Gus asked.

"We sure are," said James.

"Okay I'll leave you to it and see you tomorrow," he replied as he walked off.

"What a top bloke, he is," said James. Fletch and Jono nodded together. "Top bloke," they said.

The three girls arrived and walked straight over to the lad's table.

"These chairs taken?" asked Becky.

"Well, we were waiting for three gorgeous birds to turn up, but it doesn't look like they are coming so you may as well have them," replied Fletch.

"Charming," replied Jo as she sat down.

"What would you like to drink?" asked Jono.

"Three cokes," said Becky. "I'm pleased to see you lads drinking halves, my dad will think they're shandys."

"Come on, Jo, give me a hand at the bar," said Jono.

When he stood up, James asked the girls what they thought of Jono's outfit.

Jo looked him up and down for what seemed an age and Jono could feel the butterflies in his stomach fluttering until she responded, "I think he looks really smart, I like to see someone who stands out in a crowd and doesn't wear the same clothes everyone else does."

Jono beamed from ear to ear, and gave Jo a kiss on the cheek, thanks babe he whispered in her ear. He grabbed hold of her hand and they walked towards the bar.

"Three cokes please, mate," Jono said to a rather young-looking barmaid.

"Ice and lemon?"

"That depends," replied Jono. "Is the ice fresh or frozen?"

"I'm not sure," she said with a strange look on her face.

"Well, can you check please, because it makes all the difference."

The barmaid shouted over to her colleague at the next pump. "Lisa, is the ice fresh or frozen?"

Lisa looked across still pulling a pint. "Not sure, I think it must be frozen but ask Paul."

"Paul, have you got a minute please," she shouted to a man at a till.

Paul walked over. "Is our ice fresh or frozen?" she asked again.

He knew it was a joke but he played along. "Well, it was delivered this morning so you could call it fresh, but their again it is ice so technically it's frozen."

The barmaid looked at Jono. "So do you want ice or not?"

"Mmm, go on then but I will bring them back if the ice doesn't taste right," he replied.

She poured the drinks, put them on a tray and gave Jono the bill together with a look of bewilderment.

As they walked back, Jo pulled Jono's arm. "What were you on about fresh or frozen ice?"

Jono laughed. "It was a joke, she didn't have a clue what I was going on about, how can ice not be frozen."

Jo nodded but still wasn't too sure what he was on about.

They got back to the table and Jono gave them all the ice stunt, Fletch couldn't quite grasp it either.

"How did the fishing go?" asked Becky.

"Brill," said James.

"Shit," said Fletch at exactly the same time.

"My god, which one was it?" she asked.

James gave them the whole story, from the newspaper fire to the fish to the puking. up. to the crisp sandwiches. The three girls laughed. "Sounds like a fun day," said Jo.

"Not for us two it wasn't," replied Fletch.

"Anyway, what about the poor tramp?" asked Clare.

"He's fine, we watched through the window. I only set the top bit on fire, it was funny at the time," said Jono.

Tina came out for the first spot wearing a skirt even shorter than the previous night. The three couples talked and danced and laughed and couldn't believe it when last orders were shouted.

"Fancy coming back to ours for a coffee?" asked Fletch.

"We would love to, but my dad won't let us," replied Becky. "He's a bit strict and he wouldn't allow Jo and Clare to get into any trouble."

"Trouble?" exclaimed James. "We are thorough gentlemen."

"I know," replied Becky. "But you know what I mean."

"However," she continued. "I'm sure he'll let you walk us back to our van."

"Well, it's better than nothing," replied Jono. "But Jo, don't think you're sticking them lovely lips on mine 'cos I don't snog until the third date."

"Oh damn," she replied. "And here's me all set to snog you to death."

"I could always be persuaded," he grinned.

They left the club and walked the three girls home hand-in-hand, about fifty yards between each couple. The kiss good night lasted about five minutes and then Becky broke away and said she didn't want her dad coming out to look for them. They said good night for the last time and the lads walked home.

"My Becky has got a massive pair of knockers," said Fletch.

"You felt her tits?" asked James.

"Yep sure did, inside her blouse, and I could feel her getting all moist," he replied.

Jono laughed. "She was probably busting for a wee."

"I'm not kidding, they are like two space hoppers."

"It would be the opposite if they were bouncing up and down on you," said Jono.

"Phew just imagine I would have two black eyes by the time she had finished."

They got back and made the customary tomato soup. The dishes were still there from the night before so they used fresh ones and promised they would wash up before football in the morning. As they were lying in bed, a massive thunderstorm started. The rain was bouncing down on the caravan roof, which was soothing to hear but making it impossible to sleep. Eventually, it eased and after a long and exhausting day, they slept like babies. They woke up at 8.30 the next morning to find the sun shining through the windows.

James got up and made three cups of tea. He walked into Ryan's room.

"Bloody hell, Fletch, it's like a fog in here," he said, putting his hand to his mouth.

"Only natural body function," muttered Ryan.

"Natural? You're having a laugh, that stink isn't natural."

He got back in bed and as he did so, Jono let off the biggest loudest fart possible.

"Bloody hell, Jono, what's wrong with the two of you?"

"I think it's something to do with being sick yesterday."

"I think it's something to do with you both being smelly bastards," said James.

The door to Ryan's room was open and a loud fart could be heard through the van. Jono responded and they both laughed together. Ryan shouted to Jono, "Let's see if we can play land of hope and glory together," and farted again. Jono returned with a louder one.

"That's me done," said James. He put on his trousers and took his tea outside, leaving the door wide open to let out the smell. It was a lovely fresh spring morning, blue sky and not a breath of wind. None of them ate breakfast before a match, so once they were up and had visited the shower block, they washed all the dirty dishes that had built up and got changed into football gear.

They got to the pitch and eventually there were eighteen players to choose from, nine a side. The entertainments team of two said they would join in and make ten a side. They picked two teams and it turned out James and Gus were on one side and Fletch and Jono on the other. The girls turned up twenty minutes into the game and the three lads all seemed to find an extra yard and a bit more commitment. There was a massive puddle in one corner of the pitch from the thunderstorm the night before that Fletch had to run into to retrieve the ball. He tiptoed in but still, the water was soon all over his boots.

Jono shouted over, "You're playing too deep, Fletch." Both teams and the people on the sideline thought was hilarious.

The game finished six to three with Jono scoring three and Gus one from a free kick taken by James. They started walking over to the girls when Gus came up behind them.

"Well played, lads, good game. I can see you three are going to make it one day to a reasonable standard."

"What about you?" said James. "Have you played pro?"

"Yes, I was with Leeds up to sixteen, then Farsley Celtic which is semi-pro."

"I've heard of them," said Jono. "They are a good side."

"Yes, but you haven't got to be good to make it as a pro. You've got to be exceptional and be in the right place at the right time. I know fellas that could run rings around some of the ones that played for Leeds, but they just didn't get the breaks or their faces didn't fit."

They arrived at the touchline. "Okay, boys must go," said Gus. "We're going home this afternoon so won't be able to get you in the club tonight. You'll have to bunk in again. Nice meeting you anyway and look after these gorgeous girls."

"Cheers Gus, see ya, mate," the three lads replied.

"So, girls what do you think? We told you we were good," said Fletch.

"You're not bad but you didn't have to be that good to stand out amongst that lot," said Becky.

"But by the same token, we normally have quality players around us. We were having to do most of the work," replied Jono.

"All right don't go on about it," said Becky. "Listen, my mum and dad are having a barbecue about two o' clock and they said you three can come if you like."

"Oh no," said Jono. "I've put a roast in the oven now."

"Have you really?" asked Clare.

The other five burst out laughing. "Of course, he hasn't," said Ryan. "Yes, we would love to come."

"Good," replied Becky. "You know where we are now so we will see you later." All three girls gave their respective boyfriends a peck on the cheek and started walking away.

"Oh, and what happened to you lot being celebrities and the bouncers welcoming you with open arms into the club?" Becky shouted back.

"Gus was joking," replied James. "Do you want us to bring anything?"

"Champagne and chocolates would be nice," she replied.

"Phew, I think I'm in love," said Ryan.

"Shut up, you tosser," said James. "You've only known her two days."

"I know, but what a babe."

"Do you think she was serious about the champagne and chocolates?" asked Jono.

"Shut up, of course not. Well, I hope not anyway," said James.

They went back to the caravan, got their stuff and made their way to the shower block to get cleaned up ready for the afternoon.

The boys arrived at their barbecue to find the three girls and four adults all sat outside. The food was on the hot plate smoking away and they were each offered a bottle of beer.

"Would it be okay if we did?" asked James.

"Of course, I wouldn't offer it to you if not," replied Becky's dad. "But not too many."

The afternoon was going great with plenty of laughs and jokes until the bombshell came. The three couples were on their own whilst the adults cleared up.

"You going to the club tonight?" asked Fletch.

"Sorry, we can't," replied Becky sheepishly. "We've got tickets for a show tonight in Skeggy."

"Do you have to go?"

"Afraid so. Trust me, we don't want to. We would rather come with you, but we have no option, it was our suggestion we went to the show but that was before we met you three."

All six looked at the ground and didn't speak for what seemed an age.

"What time are you leaving tomorrow?" asked Fletch.

"Early, about nine," said Becky.

Silence again. "Fancy a walk?" asked Jono with a lump in his throat.

"Yes okay, I'll go tell me mum," said Becky.

She came back out of the van. "We've only got 45 minutes so we can't go too far."

They made it to the sand hills and separated for a goodbye snog. They walked the girls back who then got straight into the car. They waved goodbye as the car drove off.

They had all swapped addresses and promised to write and keep in touch. They also planned to meet up again in the summer. The lads walked back to their van.

"I've got an ache in my stomach," said Ryan.

"Me too," said Jono.

"You two aren't going to throw up again, are you?" asked James.

"No, am I heck, just feel a bit achy and deflated."

"I'm not surprised you feel deflated after all that farting this morning," replied James. This finally brought a smile back to their faces. "To be fair, if I was in bed with my Clare, I wouldn't get off her for two weeks."

"Two weeks? What not even for a piss?" asked Jono.

"Nope, I would just give it to her non-stop."

"In your dreams, pal," said Ryan. "But I must admit the girls at home aren't like them three."

"No, you're right they are different gravy, apart from Beverly Lewis," said Ryan.

"Bloody hell," replied James. "You and that Beverly Lewis."

They got back to the van and Jono put the kettle on.

"What shall we do tonight then?" he asked.

"Well, there's more fish in the sea," said Fletch. "Let's go to the club and start again."

"You're some skin, you are pal, Becky has only been gone ten minutes and you're moving on already," said James.

"Okay, we will let you stay in the van and dream of Clare and me and Jono will go to the club."

"Mmmm, second thoughts," replied James.

Chapter Ten

"It's talent night tonight in the club," announced Jono, "who's up for it?"

"Defo we can sing a song," replied Fletch.

"I don't know a song all the way through and I bet you don't either," said James.

There was a long pause then Fletch had the idea to sing a song his grandad had taught him and that he had sung to the lads on a couple of occasions called shine up your buttons with Brasso.

It's a song full of innuendos with an emphasis on the S in shine so it appears you are going to say shit.

"You can't sing that," said James, "we will get thrown out."

"It will be fine, it's funny as well as being a song so we will walk it."

"You're on your own, I am not getting up and singing that song on a stage," replied Jono.

Fletch sang the words and James joined in on the occasions he remembered the words.

After a couple more times, James was into it and they agreed to get up and do a double act.

"Well, I don't think it's funny and if you get thrown out and barred don't blame me," said Jono.

"Well, don't ask for a share of the winnings then," replied Fletch.

Jono tried to change the subject. "What shall we have for tea?"

"Let's have the Fray Bentos pie me mum put in for us, mashed spuds, veg and gravy," said Fetch.

"That will do me it's one of my favourites," replied Budgie.

"Right let's get everything prepared and put them on while we go to the showers," said Fletch.

"Mmmm, I don't think leaving the spuds boiling and the gas oven on while we are out is a good idea," said Jono.

That's why you have the brains and I have the good looks, but we can a least peel the spuds and get the veg ready.

They duly had everything ready to go and left for the showers.

They got to the shower block to find one shower free, Jono was first in.

The other two came free shortly after and once in and the shower block empty Fletch and Budgie began to rehearse the song again and again to make sure they were in harmony.

Jono finished up and said he was going back to put the tea on as he couldn't stand to hear another rendition of the song.

He got back to the caravan and put the pie in the oven and a light under the spuds and the veg.

By the time he had set the table, the other two were back.

"You'll make someone a lovely wife," said Fletch.

"Maybe, right I will serve it all up providing you two do the dishes and do me a favour."

"You name it, pal," said James.

"Let's have a song free tea, you two are doing my head in and you two cant hold a note between you."

"Agreed," they both said but Fletch added, "you just wouldn't know talent if it hit you in the face."

The only one who might get hit in the face is one of you two by one of the bouncers.

Jono checked the spuds and veg and opened the oven door. "How do you know when this pie is done?"

"The crust will rise about two inches," said Fletch.

"Well, how would I know if it's risen when the lids on and I can't see it?"

"Don't tell me you didn't take the lid off you idiot."

"No one told me to do that."

"Did you read the instructions?" interjected James.

"Er, no sorry."

Fletch jumped up, grabbed a tea towel and took out the tin nearly burning his hand on the hot tin.

He got the opener but in order to be able to hold it had to run it under the cold tap for a couple of minutes.

He eventually opened the lid and placed it back in the oven.

"We will give it 20 minutes and see what happens, if not it looks like being toast toppers, mash and veg providing you haven't ruined them as well, idiot," he added.

"Oh, and by the way, I take it back about you being the brains. I can't believe you were looking at the tin wondering how the crust could raise."

The piecrust eventually recovered and Fletch took charge of taking it out of the tin and sharing onto the three plates.

James put butter and milk into the pan of potatoes and gave them a good mashing as he had watched his mum do many times.

Jono was demoted to making a pot of tea.

As they began to tuck in, James stopped and said, "Just imagine if the tin had of blown up and killed us all, the headlines in the paper would say, three teenagers killed by Fray Bentos pie."

They all laughed and enjoyed the meal but especially because they had cooked it.

Chapter Eleven

They all dressed in jeans and tee shirts and splashed on the team aftershave. They got to the club and decided to go straight to the doors and try their luck, the bouncers knew they were on their own anyway.

"Evening lads," said the bouncer. "Come in but behave yourselves."

"What happened to the clown's outfit?" asked a bouncer.

Jono was about to turn around and give him some lip but James quickly ushered him into the club.

"We sure will," replied Fletch with a smile on his face.

"Wish the girls could see us now," he said as they walked in.

The comment and the memories of the previous two nights hit home and they all felt sad again and pictured the girls sat at their table. They decided to get a different table that night and James went and bought three halves. Tina and the Touch of Gold were replaced by the Jonny Bevan and the Dynamites and the first spot was good but not as good as Tina. Jono went to the toilet, as the band struck up a Booker T instrumental, time is tight which they played brilliantly.

"Come on," said Fletch. "Two birds dancing over there. Let's go ask them."

James looked over to see one petite girl and one large one.

"You can have big Bertha then, Fletch."

"No way, I spotted them first. I get first dibs."

"You're on your own then, pal."

With that, Jono came back.

"Don't sit down, Jono. You're on the dance floor with me. I've got the ideal bird for you, follow me." Fletch set off weaving his way through the tables and Jono followed behind, not knowing where or whom they were bound for. They pushed through the crowded dance floor until they came to the two girls. Fletch made straight for the petite girl and asked her for a dance. She didn't exactly give the most enthusiastic of responses, but she agreed anyway. Jono looked around and realised he had been set up. Although she had a pretty face and long dark hair, she was on the large size in both height and shape. Jono duly asked for a dance and she responded with the biggest smile. "Yes great," she said.

After three songs, Jono knew her life history. She was called Debbie, and he knew where she had been on holiday for the last three years and how she hoped to be a beautician when she left school.

Fletch and the petite one shuffled around in a circle and never spoke.

The band finished and announced bingo was to be in five minutes.

Jono thanked big Bertha for the dance and said they might do it again later in the night. Fletch smiled at the petite one and walked back to the table.

"Bloody hell," Fletch said when they got back. "She's one stuck up cow, it was like drawing teeth getting her to speak, I gave up in the end."

"I couldn't shut her up," replied Jono, "she was a really nice girl actually, just not for me. And you, you pillock, setting me up like that, but you got the short straw in the end so serves you right."

James laughed. "You and big Bertha looked like a nice couple."

"She's called Debbie, not big Bertha."

"Oh, it's Debbie is it? Not big Bertha."

With that, the bingo caller called for eyes down.

"Pick a number each and throw 10p in the middle," Fletch said. "First number out wins."

They each threw 10p in and Jono chose 26.

"I'll have 69," said Fletch. "You won't lick that."

James burst out laughing. "I'll lick it he said, I'll have number 48."

"Why do you think 69 can't be licked?" asked Jono.

The other two looked at him in amazement and laughed again.

"What?" he asked.

They never replied in disbelief.

"Our Nev went to Blackpool with his mates for the weekend and he reckons they went into a wankers bingo there," said James.

"Wankers bingo, you having a laugh budge?" asked Fletch.

"No, it true that's what he told me, it's men only obviously and the caller says right eyes down and you all start, first one to come shouts house!"

"Did he win?" asked Jono.

"No, apparently someone called house but our Nev says he just carried on."

"What for if someone has won?" enquired Jono.

"He thought it might be a false call."

All three burst out laughing much to the disgust of the all the people in the club, the most of whom turned around and said, "SHUSH."

The bingo started and they waited patiently and after about 40 numbers, the caller announced two and six twenty-six.

"Yes!" shouted Jono.

The caller stopped and announced, "Line called," and everyone looked at Jono.

"No, sorry," he said. "I was saying yes to something else."

"Have you got a line or not?" enquired the bingo caller over the microphone.

"No, sorry it was a mistake," Jono replied sheepishly.

The whole room scowled at Jono for a second time and the caller announced it was a false call and he carried on.

The three wanted to laugh out loud again when he said, "False call," but managed to keep it subdued.

"You idiot," said Fletch. "You could have had us thrown out."

"Well, just shows 69 can be licked."

James and Fletch looked at him to make sure he wasn't having them on. "Are you for real?" asked Fletch, but Jono was concentrating on scooping up the 30p.

After the bingo was finished, the compare then announced that entries for the talent competition needed to register at the side of the stage. Don't worry about the quality, it's all about the participation he added.

Fletch was up like a shot as he feared James was about to bottle it.

He registered them as the 'fly by nights' the singing duet.

As he got back, James declared he couldn't go through with it, his stomach was churning.

"Shut up, you girl, you can't bottle it now we are registered."

The compare announced there were five entries and the competition would commence in 10 minutes, furthermore each contestant would receive a beer voucher and the winner a meal for two with wine in Dunes restaurant.

James said he had to go to the toilet and ten minutes later, he still hadn't returned.

The compare mounted the stage and introduced the first act as Eddie Montgomery an Elvis impersonator.

Elvis came out of the audience and jumped onto the stage. He didn't need a wig as his hair was long and slicked back exactly like Elvis. He was wearing sunglasses and a cape and had the collar of his shirt turned up.

72

He held the mic as would Elvis and to be fair gave a great rendition of suspicious minds.

He finished with the splits and the audience were well impressed and gave him a standing ovation.

The compare came on and said let's hear it one more time for Eddie and them handed him his beer voucher.

Fletch was looking anxiously towards the toilets but James was nowhere to be seen.

He was about to instruct Jono to go and find him when he came through the double doors and back to the table.

"You okay?" Fletch asked.

"I can't remember the words."

Once we start, you'll be fine, don't worry.

Fred the magician was just completing his act off with a card trick he must have bought in the joke shop that afternoon.

The compare came on with a beer voucher in hand and said, "Come on, let's hear it for Fred."

The audience gave him a polite round of applause as he left the stage.

"Right," said the compare, "next up we have a duet from Yorkshire called the Fly by nights so put your hands together for Ryan and James."

The two went towards the stage to a mild round of applause and James looked at the exit doors and for two pins would have made a dash for them.

They climbed onto the stage and they stood either side of the mic.

The audience looked back at them but with the lights shining into their eyes they couldn't really see out.

Eventually, Fletch said, "This is a song taught to me by my grandad who sadly recently passed away." He actually passed away four years ago but he was looking for the sympathy vote.

Fletch started and James joined in.

My father's a laboratory cleaner, he cleans them by day and by night. And when he gets home in the evening, he's covered all over in…

Sssssshine up your buttons with Brasso, it's only three ha pence a tin. You can buy it or nick it from Woolworths, but I doubt if they've got any in.

Now when it comes around to Christmas, he gave me mother a fright. because instead of buying her chocolates he gave her a big box of…

Chorus

James looked up and thought he saw a woman shaking her head at her husband. This put him off a little and he missed the start of the next verse.

Some say he died of a fever; some say he died of a fit. But we know what he died of, he died of the sweet smell of…

Chorus

Now some say he's buried in a coffin, some say he's buried in a pit but we know what he's buried in, he's buried in six foot of…

Chorus

As they were finishing the last chorus, the compare was already on his way into the centre of the stage. Before they got to the last Ssssh, he took over, and thanked the boys.

Jono stood up and started to clap but quickly realised he was the only one clapping so he a stopped and sat back down.

The audience was silent as the lads were ushered off the stage without receiving beer vouchers.

They walked up to the table and sat down. "What do you reckon?" Fletch asked.

"Well," started Jono and then tried to choose his words carefully. "I could say you were bang average and try and boost your morals but I would be lying so I will just tell the truth and say you were crap."

"You havin' a laugh," claimed Fletch, "I think we've got a chance of winning and as it's a meal for two it will be me and James who will be enjoying the sweet smell of success."

"Don't get your hopes," up James said, "we didn't even get a beer voucher, so much for it's all about the participation not the quality."

The next act up was a young girl who was a contortionist mixed in with a few gymnastic moves and the last act a husband and wife who sang *I've got you babe* by Sonny and Cher and they sickly sang every word looking dreamily into each other's eyes, unfortunately neither of them could hold a note.

As the compare came to the stage to announce the winner Fletch sat at the front of his chair ready to make his way to the stage but he gave the first prize to Elvis who got up and duly accepted his voucher for Dunes restaurant with an Elvis pelvic thrust.

"Bet we came second," said Fletch, Jon and budgie just looked at each other and shook their heads.

At ten o' clock, the band struck up again and James kicked Fletch under the table.

Fletch looked up to see Debbie standing behind Jono. "Fancy another dance, Michael?" she asked.

"We were just about to go, or I would have loved to," he said sheepishly.

"It's my favourite, the band were playing a good cover version of 'Love Train' by the O Jays."

"You've got plenty of time," said James with a smile on his face. "Take Debbie up for a dance."

"Go on then, this one." He got up and followed. After two dances, they were leaving the dance floor and Debbie asked if she could have Jono's address, she could write to him. They took a detour via the bar and Debbie scribbled his address on the back of a beer mat. She gave him a kiss on the cheek and promised to write next week and with that, she went back to her table.

"Think you've pulled big time there, pal," said Fletch when he got back, "what did you go to the bar for?"

"Well, I'm not surprised," he responded. "With looks and charm like this, she naturally wanted my address to keep in touch. I notice your bird didn't come and ask you."

"Good job, I would have told the miserable cow where to go."

The compare announced it was closing time and as they were walking home, James turned to Jono. "I can't believe this afternoon you were in love with Jo and tonight you were giving your address to some big bird who could suck you up between the gaps in her teeth."

"She's got a nice set of teeth actually and anyway she's only going to be a pen pal."

The two lads burst out laughing and when they got back to the van and were disappointed to find no more tomato soup, so they settled for two slices of toast each with loads of butter.

"Right lads," said Fletch. "Let's hit the sack and we'll give it a good clean up in the morning. Not sure what time they'll be here for us, but we need to be all spick and span."

"Clare was saying they will be back for two weeks in the summer holidays," James said.

"Hopefully, if we get the all clear tomorrow, we can do the same," replied Fletch. "Imagine two weeks on our own with the girls a hundred yards away, it'd be magic."

Just before they drifted off to sleep, James asked if they all had the same ache in their stomachs.

"I think you're lovesick," said Jono. "But to be honest, I feel the same."

"Which one you fancy most Jono, Jo or big Bertha?"

"She's not big, pack it in will you with that one, anyway it's only Jo for me."

They woke next morning, had beans on toast, visited the shower block and set about cleaning up. To be fair, they hadn't spent that much time there, but they made sure it was perfect. Fletch gave it the once over, checking all the cupboards, the floors and the bins and declared it fit for a prince.

"Great," said James. "Can we walk to the shop? I need to get something for your mum."

"Good idea," said Jono. "What're you thinking?"

"Well, if I get a big box of chocolates, how about you get a bunch of flowers?"

"Sounds great," he replied.

"Oh, that's nice of you, they will appreciate that."

"Not as much as we appreciate them letting us come for four days," replied James.

Once the presents had been bought, they stopped at the deli for a sandwich, not wanting to create any more dishes to wash up. They ordered their food at the counter and eventually a young girl brought over a chicken sandwich for Jono, a tuna for James and a meat pie for Fletch and three teas.

"My sandwich is like a piece of carpet between two pieces of bread," said Jono.

"Mine is horrible, too," replied James.

"I need a chain saw to cut through this crust," declared Fletch.

They ate what they could and called the waitress over to pay the bill.

As they were walking out, Jono looked at the spotty chef behind the counter and said, "That sandwich was just like my mother makes."

The chef smiled proudly until he heard Jono finish with, "bloody horrible."

They made their way back to the van. The three cases were packed and taken outside so as not to make the van look cluttered.

The weather was cool and cloudy so they sat in the caravan waiting to be collected.

"England play Germany in a friendly next Saturday. Do you fancy watching it round at ours?" he asked.

The Fletcher household was now the proud owner of a colour television and both James and Jono both accepted the invite.

"The Germans are a good team though," said Jono, "they are so cool on the ball always seem to have loads of time."

"My grandad was in the war and was stationed in Germany for a while he says it's lovely there in fact he nearly stayed."

"If he had stayed there, would that have meant you would have been German?" asked Fletch.

"No, you Burke," replied James, "I wouldn't have been born if he had stayed there as he wouldn't have had my dad."

"Oh okay, I suppose you're right, why did he come back then?"

"He says he was going out with a girl who was half German so she only shaved under one armpit, got on his wires so he packed her in and came home."

Jono burst out laughing. "What you on about shaved under one armpit?" he asked.

"German women don't shave their armpits; didn't you must know that," said James.

"Urgh, fancy walking into the bedroom, ready for a bit of 'the other' and your bird is lying there with her hands behind her head showing two big hairy armpits, what a turn off," said Jono.

"So," said Fletch, "you want us to believe this bird of your grandad was half German so she shaved one armpit?"

"That's what he says," replied James.

"Well, I think he was winding you up."

James thought for a moment. "Mmm, you could be right, I know where my dad gets it from now."

Fletch could feel the wheels were going around in his head, he took German in school and was desperately trying to respond with something. "Could have been worse, she could have been a dairy farmer and every time he crossed the field, she shouted Ach dung, Ach dung."

All three lads fell on the floor laughing. "That's brill, Fletch," said James.

"Unbelievable, that one was good for you," added Jono.

Ryan's mum and dad turned up at 1.30 and walked into the caravan.

"Oh my God," said Mrs Fletcher. "Have you three been staying somewhere else? I expected it to look like we had burglars."

"No mum, we've been here the whole time and loved every minute. We had a good clear up this morning, but we've kept it tidy since we got here anyway."

"Only in case you brought some birds back," chipped Mr Fletcher.

"Well, I'm proud of the three of you," said Mrs Fletcher. "You might be able to come again on your own on this basis."

The three lads beamed like young kids. "That would be nice, Mrs Fletcher," said James.

The car journey home seemed like only around the corner as the lads told the stories about the club, the voice, the fishing trip (minus the tramp and his newspaper), and the football match.

"No girls involved then, boys?" asked Mr Fletcher.

"Bill," replied Mrs Fletcher. "Don't be nosy."

"Well, we did happen to bump into three nice young ladies," replied Ryan. "So expect a few letters dropping through the letter box."

"You know you said we might be able to go again?" said Ryan. "Well, what about in the school holidays for a week or two?"

"Two weeks without my baby?" said Mrs Fletcher. "I don't know about that."

Ryan blushed in front of his mates. "Behave, Mum, you could have a break from looking after me."

"Well, we'll see," said Mr Fletcher. "You're old enough now and it looks like you've had a great time and looked after the van, so I don't see why something can't be arranged."

"Having said that, I could always go with you as well, and have your meals cooked for you," said Mrs Fletcher.

The three lads looked at each other but didn't comment.

"Guess that's a no, Mary," said Bill.

They dropped James off and he said thanks again, got his case from the boot and walked into the house to find his dad watching the racing, Alex reading a book and his mum in the kitchen cooking tea.

"Aye, aye," said his dad. "It's Jules Verne, back from his explorations. How did it go, son?"

His mum came through and James gave them a rundown of the four days including meeting Clare. "It was great," he finished. "We loved every moment."

"Our James has met a bird," shouted Alex, "did you snog her?"

"Mind your own business," he replied.

Peter was speechless and looked at James with his mouth open, his son was almost a man.

"Did you get Mrs Fletcher a box of chocolates?" asked his mum trying to change the conversation.

"Yes, and Jono got flowers. They said we left the caravan so nice we could go again in the summer holidays."

"Why weren't Mr and Mrs Fletcher with you?" she asked.

"Oh, I didn't get chance to tell you they got a call had to go to a relative so they dropped us off and then picked us up on the way home."

"That's okay, son," Sheila said, "as long as you left it clean and tidy."

Sheila was so pleased James had told the truth as she had met Mrs Fletcher in the bakers on the Thursday and she told her they weren't going to be staying with them, she would have been so disappointed in him if he had not told the truth.

"Hold up," said his dad. "I've got loads of work for you in them six weeks. Don't be planning any trips around the world."

"Dad, not being funny, but if you think I'm labouring on you for all six weeks, then I am afraid you're wrong. There's girls out there expecting me to entertain them."

Alex burst out laughing. "I think he's in love."

Peter got out of his chair got James in a vice-like grip with his hand over James' mouth.

He kissed the back of his own hand and shouted in an Italian accent, "Oh baby, I love you with all of my heart!" It was a sentence from the Godfather, Peter's favourite film.

James was big and strong for his age, but still not in the same league as his dad and could do nothing about it.

"Get off, you nutter," he said. "It was just a holiday romance that's all."

The three of them almost fell on the floor laughing. James had been strictly sport and his mates until now, so to hear holiday romance come from his lips was hilarious. When they finally stopped laughing, his mum said, "You better have some good stories for our Nev. He went to get his black t-shirt to put on Saturday night and it wasn't there."

"Oh Mum, say you misplaced it and it's just turned up in a load of washing, please."

"Well, I'll try, but I don't think it will wash with him."

Even James in his tender state saw the funny side of the remark from his mother. "Nice one for you, that," he said.

He went up unpacked and brought down the washing, giving special attention to the Fred Perry.

"Quick," he said. "Just give this a good ironing and put it inside that ironing over there."

She did as she was told and James hoped he could get away with it. They were sat having tea when the door opened and in walked Nev with his girlfriend Karen.

"Right you," he said to James. "Where's my t-shirt?"

"What t-shirt?" he asked.

"You know damn well what t-shirt, the black Fred Perry."

"Neville," his mum said. "My fault, it was in amongst that pile of washing over there and I didn't see it."

"Mother, you're sticking up for him again? Just tell the truth, James, you borrowed it, didn't you?"

He now didn't want to let his mother down, so he said nothing and shrugged his shoulders in submission.

"Anyway," said dad, trying to calm the situation. "Our James is all loved up, he's got a bird."

"Well done," said Nev. "I was beginning to think you were a puff."

"Just leave me alone," said James. "I met a girl, it's no big deal."

"It was just a holiday romance," said Peter in a sarcastic voice.

It was Nev and Karen's turn to burst out laughing.

"I can't this anymore I'm off out," James said.

James went out and met up with Fletch, Jono and four of the other lads. They all wanted to hear all about the holiday and it was amazing how the stories expanded each time they were told. There were ten fish caught, different birds every night, the tramp's paper went up in flames and they had to call the fire brigade, James cracked some big guy who banged on the shower door. James told them all how much Jono and Fletch had been sick on the boat for almost three hours and how they could hardly walk afterwards.

Lemmy and Ginners thought this was hilarious. "You must be a right pair of pussies," said Lemmy, "can't even go on a little boat ride without puking."

Ginge joined in, "how rough can a boat ride be to make you sick for that long, Lemmy is right you're a pair of pussies."

"Well, talks cheap while you're here in Hardwick, I would like to have seen you two on the boat," replied Fletch.

"No problems some of us aren't wimps."

"Okay well maybe we will find out one day," he replied and made a mental note to have his revenge on Lemmy and Ginger.

Everyone was really jealous about being away having such fun on your own and wished they could have gone.

"Maybe we can hire a caravan in the summer and all have a holiday together," said Lomas.

"Not a bad idea, I will ask me mum to see if there any rentals," replied Fletch, although he wasn't convinced it would be better with 6 or 7 of them, he never did mention it to his mum, he wanted to keep it between them and the three girls.

Chapter Twelve

It was Friday and Fletch, Budgie and Jono were having a kick around on the Rec with a load of other lads. Twelve had turned up so six a side it was. When they finished, they were walking home and Fletch came up with a bright idea.

"Shall we go ice skating tomorrow? Someone told me that on a Saturday afternoon it's full of birds, apparently Quasi Modo couldn't fail."

"Pick a bird up ice skating? Are you having a laugh?" said Jono.

"Well, we will, but you might struggle, pal," he said jokingly.

"Sounds good to me," said James. "What bus shall we get?"

"Let's get the 10.30. It opens at twelve, so we'll be in plenty of time."

All three agreed they would meet at the bus stop at 10.25 the following morning. It was a 45-minute bus ride to town and as usual, the lads made their ways onto the top deck. After 15 minutes, the bus stopped and on got four girls who came upstairs and sat a few seats away from the lads. Fletch was up like a rat up a pipe and went and sat behind them.

"All right, girls?" he asked.

"We're good, thanks, you don't waste any time, do you?" said one. "You haven't given us time to warm our seats yet."

"Well, I wouldn't want you girls to miss out on my charm and good looks," replied Fletch. "No time like the present."

Fletch beckoned his mates to come over, which they reluctantly did. James sat alongside Fletch and Jono on the opposite side.

"Hi girls," said James. "Where're you off to?"

"Shopping," one replied.

"We're going ice skating. Fancy coming?" asked Jono.

"Ice skating? Never been, but you'll be fine there 'cos I've heard it's for gay blokes."

All four of the girls looked at Jono and laughed. "Just make sure you don't fall forwards or you'll dig a right hole in the ice with that nose of yours," another said. They all screamed with laughter, patting their knees at the same time.

Bugle was very sensitive about his nose and embarrassed by the girls laughing at him. "You're hilarious," he replied. "You should be comedians, I was going to tell you a joke that's so funny and you would laugh so much it would make your tits fall off, but I can see you two have already heard it."

With that, Fletch and Budgie burst out laughing. The four girls all got up together and told them to piss off before moving down the bus.

"Well done, Bugle, I mean Jono," said James. "You put them in their place."

"Who do they think they are? They were dog rough anyway."

"Never mind," said Fletch. "Wait 'til we get to the ice rink. They'll be falling over themselves to get to us."

They arrived at the skating rink and swapped their shoes for some very dodgy skates and made their way to the rink.

"I hope it's easier to skate than walk in these things," said James. "If we're not careful, we could damage our ankles in these."

"You're right," replied Jono. "Let's be careful how we go, we don't want to be injured for Kivo."

Jono was holding tightly to the perimeter handrail closely followed by James and then Fletch. Fletch was first to let go and he managed ten yards on his own.

"Come on, you wimps," he shouted. "It's easy, this."

James let go and shuffled along rather than slid. Jono did the same but then fell over laughing as he watched Fletch get too cocky and his legs went from underneath him.

"I'm not classing that as a fall," he said, looking up.

"What do you mean that's not a fall?" asked Jono.

"No, I didn't fall. It was just a bit of slippage."

"Course you slipped on ice, you dink."

James managed to shuffle around them and fell into the perimeter handrail. "Easy, you're havin' a laugh," he said. "Is this supposed to be enjoyable?"

Fletch slid on his backside to the edge and pulled himself up, as did Jono. They stood there and looked around. Everyone was going around the rink in the same direction and at various speeds. The music was pumping out and it was like a school disco on ice.

"Not bad, to be fair," said James. "It's got potential if we can just master these things on our feet."

"Now there lies the problem," Jono said as he made another attempt at skating free style.

After thirty minutes, they mastered the basic fundamentals of skating and could slide along in a fashion. The afternoon went on and the music cranked up, the lights flashed and everyone was skating around to their various abilities, trying to look cool and professional.

Fletch had spied a girl as they were going around and noticed she was stopped in the middle of the rink talking to her mates. "I'm going to introduce myself to that girl, anyone coming with me?"

They hadn't come more than five yards from the handrail at that point and neither of the other two fancied the dizzy heights of the middle of the rink.

"You're on your own, pal," shouted James. "And good luck."

Fletch set off shuffling forward like he was impersonating a steam train. He skated over to the girls but couldn't stop and he finally came to a standstill about three yards past. He tried to turn around, but his feet went up in the air and he landed on his arse. He sat there on the ice for a while not quite sure how to get up. After a while, he started to try and get on all fours, an old woman of about 70 years passed and helped him up. "You're skating beyond your capabilities, young man," she said. "Keep to the edge."

Fletch thanked her but ignored her advice. He finally made it over to the girl and stood there like a puppet with half the strings cut. "Hi," he said. "Fancy going around the ice with me?"

"You're kidding, aren't you? You look like Bambi on ice. I wouldn't be seen dead going around with you."

Fletch was in the middle of the rink; his hip and his thigh hurt like hell and he knew he had to somehow get back to the perimeter without falling, knowing his mates would be pissing themselves.

"Oh, thank God for that," he said.

"Why's that?" she replied.

"Because from over there you looked gorgeous, but your dog rough up close so I would have been embarrassed going around with you."

The girl slapped Fletch on the side of the cheek, sending him flat onto his side and he slid five yards before he came to a stop. The old woman came up alongside him again. He wanted the rink to open up and swallow him.

"What did I tell you?" she said. "Get to the perimeter before you get hurt or you hurt someone else." She pulled him up like he was a rag doll.

"Thanks, do you think you could help me to the side as well?"

The old lady got hold of his arm and shepherded him to safety. He gave her a peck on the cheek. "Now take my advice and skate around the edge of the rink," and she skated off like a professional.

James and Jono watched the old woman help Fletch to the side and him give her a peck before she skated off. They eventually managed to get themselves off the ice and stumbled over to where Fletch was sitting.

"You've pulled there, pal," said James. "I bet she is a right goer, I mean the old woman, not the bird who slapped you, whatever did you say to her?"

"I told her she looked great from the edge but dog rough up close and the next thing I know I'm sliding across the ice." The three of them couldn't move for laughing.

"You bloody well deserved a slap to be fair," James said, "good job that grandmother saved you."

"Suppose I did and to be fair she wasn't bad for an old bird, but it was a bit embarrassing having to be escorted by her to the side. Come on, I don't think this skating lark is all it's cracked up to be—my hips are killing me, and I bet I'm black and blue in the morning."

"I think you blew the quasi modo theory as well," added Jono.

"You're right, pal, never again," replied Fletch as he limped along.

They gave back their skates in exchange for their shoes and as Fletch bet down to tie his laces Jono nudged James and pointed to Fletches arse. He had a massive wet patch.

"You peed yourself?" asked James laughing.

Fletch stood up quickly grabbing his backside. "Is it really obvious, it's gone right through to my underpants, you two will have to walk behind so no one can see."

"Likely," said James, "we're going to milk this one."

"Come on, let's go to that bar the crazy daisy, our Nev says it's underground and dark and full of fanny."

"Do you think we will get served?" asked Jono.

"Apparently, it's like a converted tunnel and real dark so they might not notice."

They walked to the high street and Fletch kept getting funny looks and a young girl tugged her mums coat and said, "Look, Mummy, that boy is all wet around his bum," which Jono and James found so funny they nearly wet themselves. Eventually, they found the bar and went down the numerous steps.

It was dark, smokey, the music was loud which bounced off the curved tunnel like roof.

Jono and Fletch hid behind a pillar and James went to the bar and ordered three pints.

The barmen asked him his date of birth and James gave him one he had used a few times which made him 18 and 3 months.

The barmen gave him a doubtful look and pulled three pints fortunately not asking to see the two people he was with.

They each paid for a round with James going up to the bar each time when he could see the same bar man was free.

Nev was right, it was full of gorgeous birds but all too old for the three lads. They did however enjoy having a pint in a lovely venue ogling all the girls in short skirts.

They finished their last pint and climbed the steps to the daylight. As the fresh air hit them, they felt great they floated on air to the bus station. Just making it before the number. 215 left.

"Three halves to Hardwick please," said Jono to the driver. They got the tickets and climber the stairs to the top level and towards the back seat.

"I can't believe we have been in the boozer all afternoon and just paid halves on the bus home," said James.

They sat down and the beer and the fresh air kicked in and as the bus set off, they fell fast asleep.

The bus jolted and came to a stop, Fletch opened his eyes slowly and it took a few seconds for him to focus and realise where he was. He looked around to see Jono and Budgie still fast asleep. He looked out of the window but didn't recognise anywhere, they seemed to be inside a warehouse.

"Hey you two, wake up, where the hell are we?"

James and Jono woke up and looked at Fletch.

"Where are we?" asked Jono. "Come on quick, I think we missed our stop but god knows where we are."

They quickly came to their senses and followed Fletch down the bus to the stairs.

As they got to the bottom and saw the driver, it was difficult to work out who was the most surprised, them or the driver who was busy cashing up.

"What the hell are you lads doing on the bus?"

"We fell asleep on the back seat," replied Budgie.

"That explains it, I looked in the mirrors and thought the bus was empty, we are back at the depot now."

"Where's that?" asked Jono.

"Rotherham, where were you supposed to get off?"

"Hardwick, what times the next bus back?" asked Budgie.

"You're going to struggle, no buses go out of here anyway so you will have to walk to a bus stop and get a bus to somewhere which has a connection, you realise I should charge you for the extra distance you have been aboard, but I will let you off now please go or I will be in trouble for not doing my job right and checking it was empty at the last stop."

The three lads got off and made their way to a phone box to make the call of shame to Jono's dad to come and pick them up.

Chapter Thirteen

The two-week Easter holiday seemed to pass so quickly and they passed the time playing football on the rec, games of cards and generally hanging out at each other's houses or around the shops.

They were walking towards the rec for a kick around on the Wednesday afternoon when Fletch said there was a fair in Donnington and suggested they go one night.

"Don't you think it's a bit dodgy going there at night?" asked Jono. "You know what it will be like with the gangs around there."

Although they all went to the Donnington high school so too did 2000 other kids from numerous villages around and it was impossible to know them all especially from the older years.

"I believe it's massive this year and supposed to be brilliant but you're right we would need to go mob handed if we did," said James, "come on, it will be enjoyable."

"Let's see who's up for it and then make our decision," he added.

They got to the rec to find Ginners, Lemmy and Clanger and four younger kids playing footy so they split into two teams and carried on with the game. When they finished James asked who would be up for a visit to the fair one night.

Lemmy agreed, so did Clanger and Ginners did but not very convincingly.

That makes six of us declared James and to be honest, we wouldn't want any more or we would stick out like sore thumbs and look like we were looking for trouble.

They all agreed to go on Thursday night and get the 6.30pm bus.

James got up on the Thursday morning to find it was a lovely spring day so he decided he would wash all the windows on the house, he was never happier than when he had hose in his hand.

As they had not been washed through the winter, he couldn't believe how dirty they actually were and on completion he stood back and admired his work.

He had such a sense of achievement he contemplated starting his own window cleaning business when he left school.

Over tea, James asked his dad how much his dad considered his days' work was worth.

"Not as much as you owe me for your board and lodgings this week son, but we will call it quits" was his response.

"That's not fair, you brought me into this world so you shouldn't expect me to pay to live in the house."

"Well, you look out of the windows as much as I do so why shouldn't you wash them?"

"Peter, be fair, he's worked hard on them windows and done a great job and you wouldn't get up a ladder these days and do them and you certainly wouldn't want to pay a window cleaner so get your hand in your pocket," Sheila insisted.

Peter grunted.

"Come on, Dad, I need to start earning money it's only a year away before I can start driving lessons."

"Oh, my baby driving a car, it doesn't seem two minutes since you were learning to ride a bike," said Sheila as she walked back into the kitchen.

"I just hope you don't take after your mother; she was a nightmare when she was trying to learn, I was over the chuffing moon when she gave it up," said Peter.

"Not as glad as me and Nev, I remember every Sunday morning we had to go in the back of the car it was torture."

"I never knew mum had driving lessons," said Alex.

"Oh yes, it was horrible," said Peter. "She could coordinate her two feet trying to let the clutch out and the accelerator down at the same time and she would judder the car."

"We called it kangaroo jumps." Laughed James.

"That why she failed her first test, she was that nervous and she when trying to pull away, indicate and change gear at the same time she juddered it that much the driving instructor ended up with whiplash and had to wear a neck brace for a fortnight." Peter started to laugh.

"I can hear you," Sheila shouted from the kitchen.

"The second time, she just stopped in the middle of the high street cos she saw Betty to ask her if she was still going to bingo on Saturday, all the cars behind were beeping their horns but she was having none of it, the instructor was shouting at her to move on but she just sad she won't be a minute."

By this time, he was doubled over laughing. "On her last try, not only did she fail on her driving but also the highway code questions, on one he asked, if you were driving through the countryside what road signs would you expect to see, expecting her to say beware of farm animals or slow moving vehicles," she said, "He couldn't stop laughing tears were rolling down his cheeks."

She said, "Pick your own strawberries."

He was bent over and he said, "Can you believe it, pick your own strawberries."

He hadn't heard Sheila come up behind him and as he came back up, he got the biggest smack on the back of his head, he got the fright of his life and jumped out of his chair.

"Bloody hell, Sheila, that hurt, it didn't hurt as much as you are my feelings," she responded.

Peter rubbed the back of his head and sat back down in his chair.

"Hold on, Sheila, that's not fair, everything I said was the truth so why the crack?"

"Maybe it was but you don't have to make out as though I was thick."

"I didn't need to; you did a pretty good job of that yourself," and he regretted it as soon as the words came out of his mouth.

Sheila went to give him another smack but he ducked and shouted, "I give in, I give in."

Both lads knew it was time to do a disappearing act so Alex said he was off to his bedroom and James said he was going to Donnington to the fair with his mates.

"Come on, lads, don't leave me on my own," pleaded Peter.

"Sorry, Dad, I'm off," replied James.

"Alex, what about you?"

"Not a prayer, Dad, you're on your own."

"You be careful," shouted Peter as James walked down the hall.

"Don't worry I will, be back around eleven."

Peter sat in his chair worried he had been deserted and was all on his own.

Chapter Fourteen

James got to the bus stop to find Lemmy and clanger already there. They were quickly joined by Fletch and Jono.

"Ginge, better hurry up or he will miss the bus," said Fletch.

"I bet that's what he means to do, I don't think he was up for it," replied James.

"What a wimp," added clanger.

With that, the bus came around the corner and so did Ginners running as fast as he could. The five climbed aboard and asked the driver to hold on for a minute, he looked at his watch and then in the mirror and gave a nod.

They all asked for a half to Donnington which after scrutinising each face he duly accepted until it came to Clanger. "You look 17 to me," he said.

"I am the same age as them lot."

"Well, I was only going to make you pay full fare so maybe I should make you all in that case."

Clanger couldn't be bothered to argue so he paid up.

Ginners jumped onto the bus and the driver started to move before he had taken his fare.

They got off outside the fair ground and as the doors opened the noise of the music and screams from the rides hit them. It was fee entrance and you could either but a book of tickets or pay for each ride individually.

It was a dark night lit up by the flashing lights of the numerous fairground rides.

They decided to pay as they went not anticipating many rides would take their fancy and they were more there to see if there were any girls from school there and enjoy the atmosphere. As agreed on the bus, however, they were to all keep their eyes open for any potential trouble, as fairs like this were renowned for trouble.

Lemmy and Fletch tried their skills to win a coconut but failed miserably with Fletch claiming the coconuts were glued down.

Jono won the shooting competition where you had to shoot moving rabbits and came away the proud owner of a lovely pink teddy bear.

"You look a right burke carrying that round Donnington," said James.

"Yep rather you than me," said Ginners.

"Don't look now," said Lemmy, "but bandits at ten o'clock."

With that, they all looked around at once to see ten lads about their age or older staring at them.

"I said don't look now," said Lemmy angrily, "just pretend we haven't seen them and keep walking."

As they turned the corner, Fletch saw a ride he had seen before when he was here with his mum and dad called 'The Beast' and it was called this for a very good reason.

It was stationary with a few people queuing to get on and Fletch knew he had to act quickly.

"Quick," shouted Fletch, "that ride is absolutely brill, come on, Lemmy, Ginners, I will treat you to a go on it."

On hearing it was a freebie, they both ran after Fletch.

"You two get in the que and will go and get the tickets, do you want to go on budge," he asked.

"Yep, count me in."

Fletch made for the kiosk and asked and paid for two tickets. He went back to find Lemmy and Ginge at the front of the que, he passed two tickets to Lemmy and got hold of budgies arm, come on we will get on this cabin at the back, with that he walked back to the others with Budgie following wondering what was going on.

"What's happening, I thought we were going on as well," asked Budgie.

"Your avin a laugh, have you seen this thing in action it's a chuffing nightmare."

They looked over to see Lemmy and Ginger sat all strapped, grins on their faces, waving.

"How come them two aren't on?" said Ginger.

"Not sure, maybe it was full or more like they bottled it the pair of wimps."

Fletch was waving and smiling back as the ride started up.

Each basket was on the end of a 20ft arm which was connected to a central column which turned and at the same time the arm started to raise up in the air. The column turned faster and faster and the arm reached its maximum height.

Each time the basket came around Lemmy and Ginger were screaming and laughing and had their arms raised in the air. The column reached its maximum speed and with that, the basket started to rotate at the same time.

The screams had stopped coming from the friend's basket and as it passed in blur, they could see they were now holding on for dear life.

"Bloody hell," shouted Clanger, "that's supposed to be pleasurable."

"It looks more like torture to me," replied Jono, "they look ill."

"Why do you think I got them on before they saw it in action," said Fletch.

The ride was flashing by time after time until eventually it began to slow down. As it came to a stop, the basket came around and Lemmy and Ginger looked like they had been in a washing machine for an hour and were as white as a sheet. They slowly climbed out of the basket and ginger grabbed hold of the side before he fell over.

"You bastard, you set us up," muttered Lemmy.

Ginger was bent double and then was sick at the side of the kiosk. Lemmy looked at Ginger and baulked several times but managed to keep it down.

"You two fancy going for a nice greasy burger with loads of onions?" asked Fletch.

Ginger looked up and was about to tell Fletch where he could stick his burger but then the second wave came, he coughed it up.

Several prospective customers for the ride looked at Ginger and decided against it. One of the workers on the ride ran over with a bucket of water and brush and swilled it away, clearly it was a regular occurrence. "Can't you do that somewhere else?" he asked without sympathy. "You dirty buggers," he muttered as he got rid of the last bits.

Lemmy looked at Fletch again, and reiterated what a bastard he was.

Fletch was in his element. "Oh you two can't go on a fair ride without puking your guts up, you couple of pussies."

James, and Jono joined in the mockery. "You only went around and round a few times what's up with you?"

Lemmy tried to put a few steps together but it wasn't pretty. "I feel like I've had ten pints," he said.

Ginger bent over again but nothing came up. "Come on, boys, we can't stay here all night," insisted James.

Lemmy held his stomach and put his hand up. "Just another minute," he pleaded.

Eventually, Ginger made a move and got hold of Clangers arm. "Just help me a minute, mate, I don't feel good."

Clanger helped Ginge and Lemmy shuffled along holding his stomach until them came across the dodgem cars. "Come on, let's have a go," shouted Jono in excitement.

Ginger spotted a bench in the distance. "I'm going for a sit down, see you afterwards."

"Me too," said Lemmy.

They staggered off toward the bench but on the way, Ginger bent over again and lost some more of his tea.

James, Clanger, Jono and Fletch got in a car each and for the next 5 minutes tried to knock each other out of the fair ground. When they finished and got out of the cars, Fletch declared himself the winner much to the disagreement of the others. They were busy arguing when finally, they focused towards the bench to find it surrounded by the gang of about ten locals.

"Quick looks like they are in trouble," said Clanger as he made towards their mates.

As they all ran up, Clanger shouted, "Hey, what's going on here?"

The gang parted to reveal Lemmy stood up and Ginger sat down with blood coming from his mouth.

"You okay?" asked Clanger.

"No, he's not, the little bastard puked on my shoe look, he pointed to one black shoe and one that was a yellowy, orangery colour," said one of the mob, "and I've not finished with him yet."

"I tried to warn you," muttered Ginger.

"Where you lot from?" asked the one who looked like he could be the leader.

James took the lead. "From Hardwick, but we all go to Donnington School, so do some of you cos I'm sure I've played rugby with you, he pointed to one of the gang.

"Only when we have to and that's not very often, and just cos we go to the same school doesn't mean you're not going to get a good hiding when you're in our neck of the woods."

"Look, we've come to the fair; we aren't looking for trouble and if Ginger here puked on your shoe, I'm sure he didn't mean it."

"Well, it's too late for that, you're going to get what's coming to you," said the leader.

Ginger felt nauseous again, moaned and bent over.

One of the gang punched him on the back of the head and shouted, "Don't you dare do it again."

"Coppers," one of the gang said quietly.

With that, they started to move away from the oncoming two policeman. As one went passed, he whispered to Jono, "Ever tasted cold steel?"

Jono wasn't quite sure what he meant but he knew he didn't want to buy him a toffee apple.

The two policemen walked over and surveyed each of the lads.

"Where you lot from?" one asked.

"James took charge again, Hardwick, just down for a couple of hours to see the fair."

"Well, you boys better be careful round here; fairs are a hotspot for trouble."

One of the policemen looked at Ginger who had a combination of sick and blood all down his shirt and a swelling bottom lip.

"What happened to you, Ginger?" he asked.

"It's not Ginger, it's African Sunset."

The two policemen looked at each other with grins on their faces.

"Oh, my apologies, do let me begin again. So, what happened to you, Affffrican Sunset."

He looked at his mate and they both burst out laughing.

"I went on a ride and it didn't agree with me"

"It didn't agree with you, why did you call it names?" Both policemen laughed again.

"Yes," said Ginge, "I said it was a tosser, a bit like you two."

The smiles immediately turned to scowls, "You watch your mouth, Ginger."

They turned to go and one said, "I'd watch out if I were you lot, the natives around here eat lads like you for breakfast."

They watched the two walk away to see their shoulders going up and down as they walked, clearly laughing at the episode.

"They were a bundle of laughs," said Jono.

"True, but don't think they will rush over to give us a hand if things turn ugly," replied James. "Come on, the bus comes in 15 minutes, let's make our way to the exit and hopefully, the coast will be clear and that lot have found other things to do."

They made their way around to the exit. The park was surrounded by a 10ft high steel fence and whilst there was two ways in and out the alternative one was the opposite side and would take them into the middle of Donnington.

Lemmy was feeling a bit better but Ginger had all on walking in a straight line, his head and his mouth hurt although the bleeding had stopped.

"They got towards the exit and Clanger looked to James, what do you think, stay here inside the fair or go out into the dark."

"They will definitely spot us here so we may be better outside."

They made their way out and as they turned towards the bus stop four lads came from out of the shadows.

They all instinctively looked the other way to see three lads staring at them and appearing from inside the fair were the other three.

Ginger felt sick once more and the strength drained from his legs.

"Come on, lads, let's see how hard you posh lads are," said the gang leader.

Clanger was the biggest and hardest of the six but he knew they were no match for them. "You're a big tuff guy, aren't you, when it's ten against six, why don't me and you just get it on."

"Well, we can do that but your mates are still getting filled in as well."

Jono and Fletch weren't fighters but they would try and hold their own as best they could. Ginger wasn't a fighter at the best of times never mind after all he had been through already that night. The tension was getting to the six knowing there was no way out. The leader of the Donnington lads bent over and put his arms out. "You ready, Hardwick?" he said taunting them. They were obviously not in any rush to start the fight and clearly wanting to scare them as much as they could first, it was working.

Jono couldn't believe the hatred in the eyes of lads he had never met before.

Clanger turned to James. "I'll take him," nodding towards the leader, "you take the one at the front on that side."

"Okay," he said, "Lemmy you go towards them at the back, you three join in and do your best, we may as well go down fighting."

It was like speaking Latin to Ginners, he just didn't do things like go down fighting.

It seemed like an age but then it all kicked off. Ginners went down like a sack of spuds after the first punch not anticipating it to be followed up with a kick in the middle of his back. He curled up in a ball with his arms around his head and hoped it would stop. Clanger was holding his own and James was up against someone who was a year older but trading punch for punch.

Fletch and Jono were outnumbered and desperately trying to avoid going to ground.

James through a punch and as he turned, he noticed a red Capri pulling up at the side of the road.

The lad who had beat Ginners up now took his attention towards James and punched him from the side.

Then, from out of nowhere two knights in shining armour appeared, Nev and big Daz.

Daz wasn't called big Daz for no reason, he was 6ft 5 inches and 18 stone and although he was only 19 he was already prop forward for Donnington first team.

Daz picked up two of the Donnington lads, one in each hand, banged them together and threw them on the ground like two rag dolls.

He then turned towards the gang leader and with one punch put him on the floor.

Nev had already took the guy out who was on Fletch and turned towards the others. Their hands went up in the air and everything stopped.

"Right lads it looks like the odds have changed all of a sudden," growled big Daz.

The gang leader sat on the ground holding his jaw and Ginger also got gradually got to his feet and hobbled over towards safety near Nev and Daz.

"What do you want to do James, shall we finish them off?" asked Nev.

James surveyed the situation, five of the gang including the leader were on the ground hurt, the others were still standing but had clearly surrendered. He had taken several punches but was ok as was Clanger. Fletch, Jono and Lemmy were hurt but still standing albeit only just.

With that, Ginger punched the lad who had been picking on him since they first met as hard as he could. The lad never flinched and just turned and looked at him as though he had been hit by a fly. He wasn't however going to retaliate given the current situation.

Ginger bent over holding his hand which he had hurt punching the lad, if anything it eased the tension in the air and both Nev and big Daz smiled.

"Let's call it quits," said James looking at the gang leader, "unless you lads want to carry on. Three of them shuck their heads. The others were still nursing their injuries."

"Right, you lads have 30 seconds to get out of here or I will bang all your heads together," said big Daz.

The ten lads helped each other and walked off as fast as they could.

"Good job we turned up young brother or you could have been in serious trouble."

"I know," replied James, "what you doing here and how did you know it was us."

"I went home to get changed cos me and Daz are going to the Donnington miners welfare to see Gary Gutter and the Gutter band (Gary Glitter look alike band) and my dad said you were here, when we saw the trouble we slowed down in case it was you lot. You should know better than come to the fair here."

You're right, bad idea but it seemed a good idea at the time. Ginger caused it by puking on when the lad's shoe. "Any chance you can run him home? I don't think he's too good, are you, Ginger?"

Nev looked at Ginger who looked a mess, his hair was all matted, his shirt ripped which also had sick and blood covering most of the front. "If you think he's going in my Capri, you've got another thing coming," he said.

"Not to worry, the bus is here in a few minutes, listen thanks for helping." He shuck his brothers and Darren's hand and all his five mates did the same. They walked over to the bus stop and Nev purposely took his time getting back to the car and pulling away making sure the bus was in sight first.

The bus pulled up and the doors opened to reveal the same bus driver that had brought them to Donnington. One by one they got onto the bus and the driver looked at each of them in amazement. "Bloody hell, you lot look like you didn't have a good time."

"You could say that," said Clanger offering the same fare he had paid coming.

"I'll let you off with half this time, I feel sorry for you lot."

They all paid and made their way to the first six seats next to each other, each of the passengers on the bus looked at them and then looked away thinking they were a gang of thugs.

"I'm pissed off," said Jono.

"You surprise me," replied Lemmy.

"No really, I'm pissed off."

"We all are, why should you be more pissed off than us," said Fletch angrily.

"I won a lovely teddy and I've left it back there."

Lemmy got a cigarette packets out of the ash tray and threw it at him. "Tosser."

No one said anything else until the bus pulled up in Hardwick.

They got off and James asked, "Anyone fancy chips?"

"I've lost my breakfast, dinner and tea, so I am starving," replied Ginners.

They all agreed a fish supper would be the only way to end a bad night and they made their way cross the street to Yee's. They walked in and to find Yee bent over his fryer. As they walked in Yee looked up and began to smile.

"Ooooh, you boys look like you been in gun fight in ok cowal, you ben cheeky to someone?"

He looked at Ginners, "Oh no, you been fighting with wadese guides, or wadese brownies, ha ha, you look sick as pawwot."

Yee had stopped trying to pronounce the word 'girl' years ago and called every female a lady, or wadey.

Ginners wanted to reply by saying that's cos I'm a pretty boy but he couldn't be bothered.

Yee looked at the others who all wore cuts, bruises. "You boys no gonin to be cheeky tonight." Ha ha ha.

The boys ignored him and looked at the board to choose food.

Yee couldn't believe them. He shouted in the back to his wife, "Dongmie, (or dungmie as the boys called her) you come, cheeky boys no cheeky, quick."

Dongmie came through the beads that hung down from the architrave to prevent people seeing what was going on in the back room.

She was about 4ft 6 and had a small stool behind the counter which she used to help her see over it. She stood on the stool and peered over. She looked at each boy and then burst into a shriek of a laugh. "You no cocky boys tonight, you had good hiding?"

"Fwom goup of wadese shrieked Yee."

"Ha ha goup of wadese that's funny," replied Dongmie as she went returned into the back room she said, "no cocky boys anymore."

The boys ordered three fish suppers with curry sauce, two sweet and sour chicken and one chips and curry sauce.

Yee waited for the normal abuse and jokes that normally followed them ordering. "You no gone to say nothing cheeky?" he asked.

"Not tonight," replied James.

Yee couldn't laugh normally. He had to shriek loudly. "Not tonight cos you had good hiding from wadese guides." He was making the most of the situation.

"He is doing my head in, let's wait outside until it's ready," said Fletch.

They looked at Yee who was waving his frying spatula in the air smiling from ear to ear. They all agreed and went outside.

Five minutes later, James looked through the shop window to see Yee beckoning him in.

"Looks like it's ready," said James, so he went into the shop. "Is it ready, Yee?"

"No, I just wat to see you ugwy faces again." He shrieked with laughter again.

James went back out and shut the door. "We're going to rip him and Dungmei to shreds next time we go in, I swear."

Eventually, the food was ready. "You wat sore and finger?" asked Yee looking at them in anticipation and waiting for the normal response.

"Yes, please," they all said at the same time.

"Yey pweeze, Yey pweeze," he shrieked again, "you no cheeky boys."

"Open or wapped?" he asked and waited for the normal cheeky reply.

"Open," they all said.

Yee shrieked again.

"I swear I am going to stick that salt pot where the sun doesn't shine," whispered Clanger between gritted teeth.

They all got their food and as they were walking out Yee with both arms in the air and one hand holding the frying spatula was singing, "you no cheeky boys, you no cheeky boys," while hopping from foot to foot. The boys could see his antics in the reflection from the shop window but didn't look back to give him the satisfaction. They sat on the wall and ate their food.

"I think we made Yee's night," said Fletch.

"I am going to give it to slanty eyes and Mrs Dung next time I go in there that's for sure," said Fletch.

"Listen the micky we have took out of him let him have his moment of glory cos let's face it looking at us lot we deserved it," said Budgie.

They walked over to the wall and sat down in a line and ate their food.

"One thing, Budge, you know you said it would be an enjoyable night," stated Ginger.

"Yeah."

"All I can say is, its hard work enjoying yourself."

"Could have been worse, if our Nev and big Daz hadn't turned up we could have been sat in the hospital now, not eating fish and chips."

"We might not haver had teeth to chew with," said Clanger.

"I don't understand why they wanted to give us such a pasting, we go to the same school so why the hatred?" asked Jono.

"You're right, mate, it doesn't make sense and if I see one of them in school I will see how hard they are because I haven't finished with them," said Clanger.

Ginger wasn't sure whether the curry on an empty stomach was the right thing. "I reckon I will be shitting through the eye of a needle all day long after this curry the way my stomach feels."

"It tastes lovely but smells funny, I wonder what he puts in it," asked Jono.

"Probably a pair of his old socks," Budgie replied.

"And maybe a few pairs of Dungmie's knickers," added Fletch.

They simultaneously gasped and looked closely at the curry to see if there was any evidence of socks and knickers.

"One thing about me, I go once a day at the same time every day no matter what," stated Clanger.

"Every day," replied Jono.

"Yep, 7 o' clock every morning and my mum goes crackers."

"Why does she follow you into the bathroom?" Jono asked innocently.

"Nope, I don't get up until 7.15 and she has to change the sheets."

Now Clanger wasn't normally quick enough to set the lads up but on this occasion he excelled himself, they all burst out laughing some, especially Ginger regretting it due to the pain it caused.

Fortunately, they finished the day with a laugh although the thought of the past few words put them off finishing their food so they deposited the waste in the bin, shook hands and made their way home.

James got home and his mum jumped out of her chair when she saw the state of James. "Oh my God." She gasped. "Are you okay?"

James gave them a brief resume of the night's happenings and then said his good nights and went to bed, knackered!

Chapter Fifteen

Hardwick had won both of the last two games easily, but so too did Kivington. The next Sunday was Kivo away. The gaffer had called a Thursday night training session on the Rec at 6.00 pm, not to train as much as have a general chat about the upcoming game. They were so close and Billy wanted this as much as the team did.

It was the end of March and the school and academy leagues had finished so there were no chance of any injuries on Saturdays. They went through a few shuttles and warm up exercises and then a gentle seven a side game.

They went back to the changing room and Billy started off with a reminder to have an early night Saturday and to eat well, no pizza or chips.

"Right, lads," he said. "I'm on a plane on Monday. And when I do I want the biggest smile on my face since I scored a thirty yarder against Watford."

"Can you remember that far back?" asked Jono.

"Are you going on holiday?" asked Clanger.

"No, I have got an inch to take off the bottom of a door! Of course, I am going on holiday. Now come, lads be serious, we can do it. Don't be late Sunday, meet at the shops at 9.30. We want to be there bright and early."

As they were walking home, they came across several older lads from the 6th form milling who said they were having a game of blazing back sides.

"What the hell is blazing back sides?" asked Budgie.

"You've never heard of blazing backsides?" one asked. "It's hilarious. You can join in if you want. You lads are sporty so you should win, but you need to get a newspaper each."

Wraggy looked at Neil. "What about you, red head?"

"It's African Sunset, not red," responded Neil.

"Ha, well you would look great running down the road with African sunset hair and an African sunset newspaper stuck up your arse, come on join in."

Neil declined. "Not a prayer," he said.

Wraggy looked at his mates. "Did I tell you I once went out with a red head, she didn't have any hair just a red head." He burst out laughing as did his mates.

"Come on, lads, are you in?"

Jono looked at Fletch shrugged his shoulders and they walked across to the bins outside the newsagents. They found a load of disused local free rags that a paperboy must have discarded and salvaged one each.

"Right, what's the rules?" James asked.

"It's dark enough now so we can have the race," replied Wraggy. "Get your trousers off."

"Eh, you havin' a laugh?" asked Fletch.

"Nope, just get your trousers off, but leave your undies and shoes on."

The three watched as four of the older lads removed their trousers.

"Come on, quick," shouted Wraggy. "It's freezing here." The three removed their trousers and waited for the next instruction. "Right, the object is to roll your newspaper up. I will set this one on fire then we all light our papers up, stick it between the cheeks of our arse and run. The one who gets the furthest with it still lit and stuck up their wins."

By this time, another set of girls and boys had turned up and were intrigued to see what was happening.

"You must be crackers," said Budgie. "Who in their right mind dreamt this one up?"

"Me," replied Wraggy. "Sounds like a laugh, don't you think?" They now had an audience of eight who started to egg them on. "Okay, are you ready?" shouted Wraggy.

They all nodded albeit some of them reluctantly. Wraggy lit a newspaper. "Light your papers, boys, and may the bravest man win!"

They simultaneously lit their papers, and the seven of them set off down the high street with rolled-up newspapers stuck up their backsides and the flames starting to get bigger. A car passed in the opposite direction and nearly crashed as the driver looked on. The flames were even higher as the seven then passed an old woman walking her dog. She stood still with her mouth open and had to hold onto a lamppost to prevent her from falling over. As the flames got closer to their skin, one-by-one they stopped and dropped the burning papers until it was only Wraggy and James left.

James could feel the heat, but he wasn't giving up. Another car passed and sounded his horn in disbelief as the two passed him. Finally, James felt the flame lick his skin and he quickly dropped the paper. Wraggy kept on going screaming with delight until he finally stopped and jumped up and down with his hands in the air. They all gathered back at the starting point to the claps and shrieks of the audience.

"That was unbelievable," one said.

"Absolute madness, if you ask me," said another.

Wraggy, full of pride, declared himself the blazing backside champion and decided from then on, he was going to challenge anyone to try and take the crown off him on a monthly basis.

James, Fletch and Jono put their trousers back on. "You can keep your title," said Jono. "It's mad," Fletch agreed.

"Well count me in next time, Wraggy," said James. "You only just beat me and that's 'cos you rolled your paper up tight. I never thought about that."

"Well, bring it on, Budgie, we'll have the rematch in a month."

The lads walked home. "That Wraggy has got a screw loose if you ask me," claimed Fletch.

"You're right. It was probably funnier to watch than take part in though," replied Jono. "Did you see the woman with the dog? I thought she was going to pass out."

"Yes, but imagine looking up and seeing seven lads with flaming newspapers stuck up their arse coming for you, you would pass out as well!" They all laughed and went their separate ways.

Chapter Sixteen

It was Saturday night and it was Kivo away in the morning and James couldn't believe he was at home on his own. This didn't happen very often in fact he couldn't remember the last time he was in on his own. His mum and dad had gone with Betty and Ken to the working man's club. Alex had gone to Snid's birthday party in the afternoon and then was staying at his house for the night and Nev as usual was either out with Karen or his mates.

James had his night planned out, a nice soak in the bath, watch Morecombe and Wise then an early night ready for tomorrow's game.

He laid in the bath and just listened to the silence; it was heaven. He thought about the match tomorrow and then whom he would vote for player of the year. Billy had handed out the voting slips after the last game. There were twenty votes, fifteen for the squad, one each for Billy and his assistant Mike, one for George the Hardwick club chairman, one for Rex the club secretary although both of them only saw 50% of the games and one for the clubs most loyal supporter, Joyce, or Auntie as everyone called her who stood on the line come rain or shine wearing either a head scarf or a rain hood to protect he hair.

The slip had to be handed in tomorrow and to prevent a player voting for himself, which had happened in the past, each slip had the person's name on the top.

James had already made his choice, Jono, not because he was his mate but because he was a quality player who had had a great season scoring 43 goals. He could have voted tactically for someone who didn't have a chance of winning as his vote could prevent him from voting but James wasn't like that.

It probably didn't matter anyway because there was only Billy who saw and counted the votes so he could fiddle it to suit who he wanted.

His thoughts then drifted to Clare and he wondered if he would be the first girl, he did it with.

One thought lead to another and before long James started doing what 16-year-old lads do when they are in that frame of mind. He was suddenly brought back down to earth when he heard the front door slam.

"Who's that?" he shouted down.

"James, it's me what the hell are you doing in?" said Nev.

"Having a bath."

"Bugger," he heard Nev say.

Neville had been going out with Karen for six months although they had known each other since primary school. Her house was a busy as theirs as Karen had an older sister and a younger brother. Their time alone was, therefore, restricted to the back of Nev's Ford Capri.

It was a very nice car but only being two doors meant they had to be contortionists at times.

Nev had picked Karen up at six, took her for a meal at the Red lion although the food there was not the best it was local. He knew Alex was out for the night, His mum and dad were going to the club and James was always out on a Saturday night so they could have a comfy couple of hours on their own for a change.

They were giggling like young kids as they walked up the path and Karen pinched Nev's buttock as he opened the front door. As he shut it, he heard splashing water from upstairs and James shout, "Who's that?"

They both walked into the living room and Nev turned on the TV. "I don't believe it," he said to Karen, "just two hours on our own that's all we want, just two hours."

"We will have to go away for a long weekend," she replied, a smile came back onto Neville's face.

James came into the room in his bath robe. "I bet you expected to have the house to yourselves, didn't you?" he said sarcastically. "But don't let me spoil your fun just pretend I'm not here."

"What you doing in on a Saturday?" Nev asked.

"I had a nice quiet night planned before the game tomorrow but looks like we're having a threesome now." He saw the embarrassment on Karen's face so he changed the subject. "Morecombe and Wise, shall I turn it over?"

After it had finished James made himself a cup of tea and announced he was going to bed. He laid there and he couldn't believe the silence again, it was the first time he had been in the bedroom alone for a long, long time so he picked up where he had left off in the bath and slept like a baby.

Chapter Seventeen

It was all down to the last game: Kivo away. Hardwick only needed a draw and Kivington a win by two clear goals but what was really at stake was the prestige of winning. The bitter rivalry between the two villages had been built up over many years by generations before them. It was like Celtic versus Rangers or Manchester United versus Liverpool.

Budgie woke early that Sunday morning, contemplating the game ahead and the butterflies were fluttering in his stomach already. Nev opened the door and picked his head around. "Make sure you beat them, James."

"We will do our best, make sure you're there."

"Don't worry I'll see you there," he said. "Meeting a few of the lads for breakfast at the café."

"They coming as well?" asked James.

"Yep we're going mob handed."

"No, but—"

With that, he was gone. When he was ready, James got up and went downstairs to find his mum doing the washing.

"Morning, son," she said. "Fancy a nice cooked breakfast?"

"No, thanks," replied James. "Not before a match, you know."

He was downing his second glass of water when his dad came into the kitchen dressed in a scruffy pair of tracksuit bottoms and an old t-shirt. Sheila put the kettle on. His dad looked hungover. He was only 45 years old, but at that moment, he could have passed for 60.

"God, you look rough," James said.

Peter looked at him but said nothing. To Sheila, he said, "A bacon sarnie would be lovely?"

"A bacon sarnie would be a miracle," she replied. "Seeing as we have no bacon."

"You're kidding, no bacon on a Sunday morning?"

"Why don't you have a bacon sandwich with no bacon?" asked James.

"Why don't you run to the co-op and get some bacon?" replied his dad.

"Can't, sorry, got to save my energy for Kivo away. You coming to watch?"

With that, Alex breezed in. "Bloody hell you look like a bear's arse," he said to his dad.

Alex was the only one who could get away with that, but his dad gave him a light scutch and followed it with. "You cheeky little bleeder. Sorry, lad," he said to James. "Got work on the allotment and then then the usual lunchtime beverage with my mates, but make sure you beat them scum."

"What you doing back so early?" Sheila asked Alex.

Snids going to his nans in Leeds so they were leaving early.

They all went into the living room and sat down with a cup of tea.

"Hey, did I tell you about the Irish man at work last Friday?"

"Is this a joke?" asked James.

"No, I promise it's a true story. I was in the stores on site talking to Norman the store man—"

"See I told you it's not true," James cut in. "Norman the store man!"

"Swear to god that's his name. Anyway, Seamus, one of the Irish ground workers, came in and said, 'I've something in my eye, do you have anything for it?" Norman went to the first aid cupboard got out an eye bath, poured some solution in it and gave it to Seamus. But Seamus said, 'Cheers,' and drank it! Me and Norman looked at each other, we couldn't believe what we saw. The best thing of all, I saw him ten minutes later and asked him how his eye was, and he said it was fine and that stuff Norman gave him worked a treat!

"Dad, don't tell lies," said James. "It's one of your tall stories."

"I'll say it again, it's true."

"Right, I'm off," said James. "I'll see you later."

Kivington village was two and a half miles away by road or one and a half miles on a dirt track over the fields, but it may as well have been on another planet. The kids went to a different school and rarely came eye-to-eye unless it was school versus school or team versus team. Other than sport, rarely would either set of kids venture into foreign country. There was no need and it wasn't worth the risk.

Hardwick met outside the shops as they always did for away games. The adrenaline was pumping higher today and lads were cracking jokes trying to ease the tension.

Jono took the kit home to be washed each week. His mum charged two pounds. Jono's dad brought him to every game so it was easy to let him take the kit home to be washed and then bring it back. The trouble was Jono took after his father, who was nice, but dim and after getting lost on route to two away games, Billy had insisted they wedge them in the middle of the convoy of cars. Turning up without Jono was bad enough, but without the kit as well took the biscuit.

As usual, on this occasion, they were late and Billy was pacing up and down. "Where is the bloody halfwit?" he exclaimed.

"Probably thinks it's at home, knowing him, Gaffer," said Stubby. "Why don't you drop him and teach him a lesson?" Stubby had a better chance of playing if there was no Jono.

"Yeah, that'd be wise," replied Billy, tongue-in-cheek. "Jono was one of the best players on the team. He could beat all eleven of the opposition and go back and beat them again if he wanted."

With that, Alfred Johnstone's car came around the corner and everyone gave a sigh of relief. Except Stubby.

"Let's get going everyone," Billy called out. "We know where it is, so we'll see you there."

The ten cars set off. They arrived in the club's car park and the first to the changing rooms was Clanger, closely followed by Billy. They tried the away changing room door, but found it locked. The Kivo manager, Kev, a rival of Billy's for years, came out of the home dressing room.

"Sorry, Billy," he said. "There was a leak in the showers and the council have locked them up. You'll have to get changed in your cars."

"What about sharing yours?" asked Clanger.

"Sorry, no room in there," he said with a smirk on his face.

Billy looked at him and felt like cracking him one. "You expect me to believe that old chestnut, Kev?" he asked.

"Phone the council if you don't believe me," he responded. "Nothing I can do about it," he said.

Billy smiled and walked away. "We'll have the last laugh," he said, loud enough for Kev to hear.

"He's lying," said Clanger.

"He is one lying bastard," replied Billy.

Billy didn't allow any swearing from his team on or around the pitch as he tried to encourage as many spectators as possible from the village, but on this occasion, he couldn't help himself. He knew in the battle of wits it was one nil to them. "Right, lads. Change in the cars. I'm afraid the changing room is out of order."

A loud groan went up. "You having a laugh?" shouted Lemmie. "It's freezing."

"Don't argue. Nothing I can do about it." Billy read out the team and told them to get ready before he had his chat.

Mike the assistant manager emptied the kit bag in the middle of the car park and it was a free for all whilst they tried to snatch the best items of kit.

Once they were all ready, Billy called them around. "It's been a long season and it all comes down to this one game. Win this and we show this lot who's best. Make it clear we are not playing for a draw, we go out to win, no matter what." His talk lasted five minutes and the lads listened without comment. He waited 'til the Kivo team were on the pitch putting up the nets before he finished with, "Do we want to win?"

"Yes!" they replied in unison.

"I said, do we want to win, Hardwick?"

"Yes!" they shouted again.

"Come on, then!"

They all shouted as they broke away, storming the pitch.

Chapter Eighteen

Twenty more Hardwick supporters turned up just before kick-off. Nev and two of his mates came shortly after, making a decent support for the way team. Kivo had about forty on their sideline, so they were in for a good hiding if it all kicked off. That is, until the pubs and clubs opened when a lot of the home fans would disappear.

Keith Bradley had been assigned to the game to referee. He was one of the best and most respected refs in the area and had been chosen for this match due to its importance and the many possibilities of trouble. It was normal for a man from each side to run the line and Keith was assigned a bald-headed bruiser from Kivo and one of the dads, Tony, from Hardwick. It was expected that they would probably be biased, but the ref would overrule their calls when required.

The game kicked off and within the first five minutes, Budgie went through their midfield playmaker with a two-footed tackle. Several players ran over and spectators spilled onto the pitch, shouting abuse. The ref diffused the situation and gave Budgie the sternest of warnings, but to the dismay of the home team, no yellow card.

The first half ended nil-nil. The home supporters had been intimidating the Hardwick players on their side of the pitch by hurling abuse, sticking legs out as then ran down the wing, and telling them how they had slept with their mothers the previous night. The Hardwick players had done as instructed and ignored them.

Jono had been on the wing and was having his normal brilliant game, but the manager of Kivo had put a man-to-man marker on him; a thug called Nigel Flinders who was getting angrier every time Jono went past him. Intimidation by him and his supporters hadn't worked and the more fun they made of his big nose, the more determined he was to take Flinders to the cleaners.

The Hardwick linesman had been on the side with his supporters for the first half and given several dodgy off sides. The Kivington supporters had hurled abuse a him from across the pitch and it was customary for the linesman to swap sides for the second half. The ref went over to Tony. "May I suggest you don't swap sides second half, it could turn a bit nasty over there."

Tony wasn't the biggest or bravest of men but he was not one to back down either. "They don't scare me," he said, "thanks but I am not letting them lot think I am scared of them."

The ref shrugged his shoulders and walked away.

Stevie, the Hardwick centre forward, had done as instructed by Billy and had kicked and bullied the Kivo twin centre halves for 45 minutes. He had received a booking for elbowing one in the nose as they jumped for a corner and Billy took him off at half time before he got a second. The two centre halves breathed a sigh of relief when they saw he wasn't returning for the second half and even managed a slight grin when they saw his tall skinny boy band type replacement. They had never seen Crofty before.

The ball came out from the Hardwick defence to Tomo on the right who passed it down the line to Jono. He turned inside, beat one and laid it into the path of Crofty, 25 yards from the Kivo goal. He feigned one way, went past one defender, twisted past the second and then sent the keeper the wrong way to slot it in the bottom corner.

The team, Billy, and all the supporters went wild, running over to Crofty who was on the ground with players on top of him.

As the game restarted, the ball went high into the Hardwick half and immediately, Tony the linesman put the flag up for offsides. The ref blew and the Kivo supporters went ballistic.

A mean-looking bystander came up to Tony. "You put that flag up once more and I'll stick it right up your arse." He spat.

Two Hardwick supporters, along with Nev and his mates, walked over towards the side where Tony was and were ready to jump in if necessary.

Five minutes later and the flag went up again, but the referee ignored the call and shouted, "Play on!"

The mean bystander, however, wasn't interested and marched towards Tony. Nev, his mates and the other fans walked down the line and several Kivo supporters started towards them. After some pushing and shoving, threats and abusive language, the ref blew up and stopped the game. He took the flag from the linesman and informed him he would sort it out from then on.

The Hardwick men walked towards their side of the pitch with shouts of "Get over there, you cheating bastard!" from the Kivo fans.

Tony turned around and stuck two fingers up.

One of the Hardwick heavies walked up to the Kivo linesman and took the flag off him. "If we can't have one, neither can you," he shouted.

The Kivo linesman didn't argue. By the time his cavalry had got to him, it would have been all over.

The game resumed and two minutes later, Crofty picked up the ball just inside the Kivo half. He beat three players before side footing it around the keeper. Hardwick went crazy. It was two-nil and the league was almost theirs.

With twenty minutes to go, Hardwick were being pressed by Kivington. They knew one goal and they were back in it. Budgie tackled their midfielder and won the ball. He ran forward, dummied one and went past another. He then had two options. He had Jono to the left and Crofty to the right, both with equal opportunities. In a spilt second, he chose Jono, a choice that would haunt him for a long time.

He kicked the ball into Jono's path. Jono trapped the ball turned one way, then was about to shoot when the full back Flinders came in and hit Jono from the side. The crack of bone could be heard on the side-line. Jono dropped to the floor but made no sound.

Some of the Hardwick team ran over some to see how Jono was, while the others went have a go at Flinders.

"You dirty bastard," said James as he swung a punch at Flinders.

Flinders ducked and swung back but there were so many people involved, pushing and pulling. The spectators were in it, too, but most had forgotten about the reason for the fracas which was Jono.

Eventually, they calmed down. Jono came around enough to see the consequences of the tackle. Blood seeping out of his sock and his leg was clearly a mess.

"I can't look," said James, and he walked over to the side-line.

Fletch joined him. "I don't believe it," said Fletch. "That dirty bastard did that on purpose."

They sat on the wooden bench on the sideline and didn't say another word until Megan walked up with her dog, Buster.

"What's happened?" asked Megan.

James looked up. "What're you doing here?" he asked.

"Just brought our Buster for a walk and thought I'd watch the match. What's happened? Why aren't you playing?"

She had two reasons for coming: one, to give Buster a good walk over the fields, and two, to see James in his shorts.

"Megan, your Michael has been hurt. Go home as fast as you can and tell your mum and dad but don't go over and see him," James added. "I think he's got a broken leg."

The cold air and the shock of seeing Jono on the floor had made James feel shivery, but all of a sudden, he felt a nice warm feeling on his leg. He looked down to see what could possibly be causing this warmth and there was Buster with cocked leg, peeing on his shin, the steam rising in the cold air.

James jumped up. "You dirty—" he said. He was about to give Buster the biggest kick up his backside when Megan yanked him away.

"He thought it was the leg of the bench," she said in his defence.

The steam was still rising, and the information went quickly down the sideline bringing a much-needed smile to everyone's sad and concerned faces. "He shouldn't even be on the field," said James. "It says no dogs allowed."

"Sorry," she said. "I'll get off and tell my parents. Tell Michael I was here and I've gone back home."

She was all of a fluster, worried about her brother and also how she had ruined her relationship with James before it had even started. She ran off dragging poor buster behind her.

Billy was at Jono's side with the trainer, Jack Watson, who had a numbing spray and a bucket full of cold water. Neither was of any use in this situation. Someone had been sent off to ring the ambulance.

The ref declared that the match was abandoned and asked all the players to leave the field and the supporters to go home. He could sense that longer they were here the more the tension would build up.

Flinders and several more passed James and most of the Hardwick team as they went to the dressing room. He was talking and grinning to his mates.

"I'll knock that smile off your ugly face," shouted James.

"Anytime, tosser," Flinders replied, sticking two fingers up.

James jumped up to run at him. "I'll kill you, Flinders," he shouted, but was stopped by several of his teammates.

"He's not worth it," said Lemmie. "Let's not make it worse."

"I'll make it worse for him," vowed James. "He isn't getting away with that."

The Kivington lads walked off as the ambulance arrived and drove onto the pitch. The paramedics got out and surveyed his leg.

After a few moments, Billy came over. "It's not good," he said. "As we thought, it's definitely broken."

Everyone looked at the ground. "What's happening with the result?" asked Crofty after a few moments.

"Not sure, we'll have to wait and see."

"Do me a favour please, go and get changed and no trouble, you hear me? We don't want the ref giving us bad comments in his report, everyone understand?" They all reluctantly agreed. He turned to the adults that were still there. "You lot, please stay with them and make sure they don't get into any trouble."

Neville was there and promised to look after them.

"Gaffer," said James. "Jono's sister was here, she has gone home to tell her parents."

"Good," he replied. "I'm going in the ambulance with Michael, I'll phone them when I get to the hospital." With that, he walked back over to Jono and the lads returned to the cars to get changed.

Neville drove James home, but they didn't speak the whole time. James was thinking about the pass he didn't need to make and also planning his revenge on Flinders. Nev dropped him off at home and said he was going for a drink with the lads but would be home for two. James walked into the house to find his mum in the kitchen and Alex watching TV. He went straight to his room. His dad would be back from the pub in half an hour and he only wanted to go through the story once.

At 1.55pm, he walked downstairs as his mum was dishing up.

Chapter Nineteen

Peter Burgess was a popular person in the village, always had a story to tell and loved the odd practical joke and a few pints with his mates. This Sunday, however, his mates at his local, the Red Lion, had arranged for the joke to be on him for a change.

He always came into the pub at 12.30, had four pints and left at 1.50 as Sheila had his dinner ready to put on the table at precisely 2.00 and he daren't be late.

Everyone in the pub was primed ready. He walked in on time ordered his usual and sat down with his three mates for a game of dominos. The time passed and when it was 1.30 and Pete was on his fourth pint, big Roy said he was bored of fives and threes and did they fancy a game of pinchy pinchy?

Right on cue and as rehearsed, Ronnie replied, "What the hell is pinchy pinchy?"

"Well," said Roy. "On everyone's face, there are ticklish points and when you lightly pinch them you can't help but smile. You go around in the circle taking turns pinching the man to your left twice and as you do so you say the words, pinchy, pinchy. If you smile when you're pinched, then you're out. We will throw in 50p a man. The last man standing takes all."

The four men on the table next to them who had stopped what they were doing to listen and wanted to join. As previously arranged, Stan sat at the bar shouted over, "Count me in as well, boys!"

"What a load of rubbish," said Pete. "Grown men sat in a pub pinching each other's cheeks!"

"Not just cheeks," replied Roy. "It can be the nose, chin or forehead—you've just got to find the ticklish points."

They all sat around the table with big Roy to Peter's right and in the pot was four pounds.

"Go on, count me in, then," said Pete as he threw in a 50p coin. "But don't blame me when I walk out with your money."

"I'll start," said Stan. He turned to Paul on his left and lightly pinched one cheek then the other but got no reaction. Paul then turned to Phil and did the same thing but again, no reaction. It got around to Roy's turn and he turned to his left and gave Peter's nose a pinch and one to his forehead. He didn't move a muscle.

After two rounds, Paul couldn't hold it back and started laughing. One by one, over another four rounds, they each started to laugh and, on each occasion, Pete looked at them in disbelief.

"I just can't see why it makes you laugh. There must be something wrong with you," he said.

Gradually, they all laughed and it came down to Roy and Pete and after another six goes each, Roy gave in and burst out laughing when Pete pinched his chin.

Pete looked at the clock, it was ten to two. He got up, scooped up the money, finished his pint and said, "Well, that's the easiest four quid I've ever made and you lot must be out of your trees. I'll see you later."

When the door shut behind him, the pub was in uproar with people giving high fives and bent over laughing.

Peter walked the two-hundred- and fifty-yards back home. On his way home, he saw a young girl coming the other way, walking her dog. Peter smiled as he passed her, but she looked at him in amazement. He didn't see her walk straight into a lamp post immediately after she had gone past him turning her head as she past.

A car coming the other way peeped its horn and a young lad leaned out of the window and shouted something Peter couldn't understand. *Must know me,* he thought to himself.

Peter walked into the room as Sheila emerged from the kitchen with two plates in her hand. When she saw him, she stopped, her jaw dropped and she looked at him in disbelief.

"What on earth have you been doing?" she said as she put down the plates, not wanting to drop them.

Alex and James looked up and burst out laughing.

"What?" exclaimed Peter.

Sheila joined in the laughter, bent double. Alex was holding his stomach and pointing at his dad's face.

"You're all as stupid as those lot in the pub. What's so funny?"

"Go and look at yourself in the hall mirror," said Sheila in between laughs.

Peter walked into the hall and looked in the mirror. What he hadn't realised when they were playing pinchy pinchy was that Roy had been sitting right next to a very full ashtray into which he had been dipping his hands. Each time he pinched various parts of Peter's face, he left black ash marks until it was covered and his face looked like the ace of spades.

Peter looked into the mirror to see his face was completely black. "The shower of bastards," he said. He looked again and saw the funny side and joined in the laughter. "I'll get my own back," he said. "I'll get my own back." He went into the kitchen to wash it off and found the family unable to contain their emotions. Alex was on the floor holding his sides, Sheila was sitting down with tears streaming and James just stood there, pointing at his dad's face.

They heard the front door open and Peter made to go to the kitchen before Nev came in, but James blocked his path and Sheila jumped up and guarded the door. "No way are you doing our Nev out of seeing this," said Sheila.

Nev walked in. "What's all the—" He didn't finish his sentence as he looked at his dad's black face.

"They've played a trick on him in the pub," said James. "He's walked home and didn't even know."

"Right, you've had your fun. Now I'm washing it off. I don't care what you say."

"Hold on, Dad," said Alex. "Let me just get my camera and take a photo." He ran upstairs and got the Polaroid camera he had for Christmas.

"You can take my photo on one condition: it doesn't go out of this house, okay?"

They all reluctantly agreed and once the photo had developed, it was put in prime position on the mantelpiece above the fire.

Lunch took twice as long to eat because both in between and during mouthfuls each one of them would look at the photograph and burst out laughing.

"I'm pleased you find it amusing," said Peter.

"Amusing, it's frigging hilarious," said Alex.

"Hey pack it in with the language," said his mother. "But you're right I haven't laughed as much as that in years."

After lunch and once everything had calmed back down, James recited the morning's happenings. It had brought him back down to earth and the thoughts of how he had passed to Jono and not Crofty flooded back. "I'm just going to lie down for a bit," he said, and he retired to his room. He wished he could walk down to Clare's and just chill with her.

If only I had passed to Crofty and not Jono, he thought.

Chapter Twenty

At five o' clock, James came downstairs and said he was going down to Jono's to see if his parents were back from the hospital. He arrived at the house and Mr Johnstone answered the door.

"Come in, James, come in, mate," he said. "Go through to the living room." He went through to find Mrs Johnstone in tears on the sofa with Megan. Megan obviously wasn't expecting James and was shocked to see him standing there whilst she was in such a state. She immediately made her apologies and went upstairs.

"Would you like a coffee or tea?" asked his dad.

"No, I'm fine," James said. "How's Michael?"

"We have just gotten back," said his mum. "He has broken it in two places. They might need to pin it and they are taking him down to theatre at 6.00. They say he will be in there at least two hours and by the time he gets over the anaesthetic, it will be too late so they are going to telephone us later." She started crying again and added, "I don't think he will ever play football again and you know, there were two scouts from Sheffield there this morning looking at him, so Billy was telling us."

James wasn't aware of the two scouts. Billy obviously hadn't said anything in case it affected how anyone played. He tried to say the right words, that he was a tough kid, that he would be back, but he knew he would never be the same after this.

He was saying his goodbyes as Megan came down the stairs looking like she had had a makeover.

"Sorry for what Buster did this morning," she said.

"It's no problem, I just couldn't believe it when I saw all the steam. I can laugh about it now. See you," he said as he shut the door.

He walked back feeling worse than he had before. *Why didn't I pass to Crofty?* he thought. He was approaching the shops where he found the Riley twins and their gang milling about. They would have normally picked on a lad on his own, but they knew not to mess with James.

"You all right, Budge?" asked Sean. "You look as sick as a parrot."

James was ready for any sarcasm and would have dropped the first person who said something out of turn. "I am," he replied. "We played Kivo this morning and one of their thugs broke Jono's leg in two places, and he meant to do it."

"I hate those Kivo scum," said Steven.

"I feel like going down there and finding the bastard," replied Budgie.

"There's a bus in ten minutes. Let's go see if we can find him," said Baker. "Chances are some of them will be 'round the shops."

They all quickly agreed and James was certainly up for it. The bus turned up and they got aboard.

"We'll get off at the top of the high street," said Sean. "And look around first, we don't want to get off into the middle of the high street."

The adrenalin was pumping and although they were nine strong, they were in enemy territory and didn't know who or how many they would come across. They also didn't know the back streets and alleys that made up the Kivington estates. God help them if they got lost or worse, split up. James could tell a couple of them were beginning to regret the hasty decision to jump on a bus and come to Kivington. It was still dusk and they walked down the high street with no one in sight. All the shops were shut except the chip shop and the pizza place. As they turned the corner, they spied five teenagers outside the chip shop.

"Quick," said James. "We don't want them to see nine lads they don't recognise."

They hid in a shop doorway and looked for a route. Next to the shop was a road which undoubtedly would allow them to turn right further down and get closer to the chip shop without walking down the high street. They peeled away one by one and sure enough, eventually they came back to the high street almost opposite where they needed to be.

James looked across and the blue fluorescent light of the shop helped him recognise the brown mop of hair and flat nose of Flinders. They were directly outside the chip shop with a bus stop to their left.

"It's him," James whispered.

"Let's get them while there are only five," said Sean.

"Wait," replied Budgie through gritted teeth. "Let's just make sure there's no surprises around the corner."

There were no customers in the chip shop, no one at the bus stop and the high street was clear in both directions. Budgie spotted a bus coming in their direction that would certainly stop outside the chip shop.

"Right lads," said James. "As soon as the bus pulls up, you take four, Sean, and come in from the right. I'll take four and come in from the left. One more thing," he added. "The lad in the blue jacket and long hair is mine, everyone understands?"

They all nodded. As the bus pulled up, the nine made their way across the road and stayed out of sight until the bus pulled away. Once it was past, they attacked from both sides. The Kivo lads didn't know what had hit them. Budgie was one-on-one with Flinders and whilst they were evenly matched, Budgie had the will and the determination on his side.

Inside the chip shop, Gregorio was preparing fish, ready for the influx of customers when the pubs kicked out. He heard the bus pull away and then the commotion that ensued. He quickly realised the scale of the brawl and, not wanting it to spill into the shop, he dried his hands and ran into the back to phone the police. The police station was less than a mile away.

Flinders went down and then suffered a few more blows with Budgie on top of him. Budgie stood over Flinders, who was groaning as he rolled onto his side and Budgie stood on his knee, hearing the ligaments tear.

"That'll teach you, you bastard, see how you like being injured for the next six months."

Flinders had clearly had enough. He was bleeding from his nose and mouth and trying to get up, but his knee wouldn't let him. Budgie looked around to see the rest of the Kivo lot were also well beaten. He heard the police siren in the distance and shouted, "Come on lads, let's get out of here quick!"

They naturally set off in the direction from which they came. In hindsight, it was a big mistake. If they had thought about the escape, they would have run in the opposite direction and could have turned right after 200 yards and within five minutes, they would have been on the track over the fields to Hardwick and if anyone chased after them, they could only come from behind.

Chapter Twenty-One

Gregorio's son, Costas, was in the back when he heard his father on the phone to the police. He quickly went into the shop and looked over the counter. The shop front was almost all glass. He recognised James Burgess, standing over Flinders and saw other Kivo lads on the floor with boys he didn't recognise. They then took off when the police siren could be heard, leaving the Kivo boys behind.

He saw Flinders trying to get up, but as he did so a blonde-haired lad came past the window and booted him in the side of the head before running off to catch up with the rest. The kick sent Flinders reeling sideways. Costas heard the thud on the metal at the bottom of the glass as his head hit it. Costas had played in the match that morning and immediately knew it was Burgess and his mates after revenge. He thought he recognised the blonde-haired lad who kicked Flinders, but not from the match.

He ran out of the shop and saw his five mates in various positions on the floor or trying to get up, they were clearly in no state to retaliate further, He looked at Flinders and saw he was out cold, blood oozing from his head. There was nothing he could do. The police siren was getting louder. He ran off into the estate in search of anyone who could help find the lads involved. He quickly found four of his mates on a street corner and it didn't take long to convince them to join him.

As they were passing the Forge pub, four men were stood outside. They had been spectators at the match that morning. After quickly explaining to them what had happened, they needed no persuasion to join in and seek revenge. The police pulled up outside the shop to find four lads standing but bent over in pain. One person was lying motionless on the ground.

They made straight for him and slowly turned him over. He was clearly unconscious, and blood was coming from his head.

"Quick, get on the radio and get an ambulance ASAP," one said to the other. He checked his pulse to find him alive, but clearly in a bad way. They got a blanket from the car and rolled it up and put it under his head. One of the policemen took off his jacket and put it over Flinders.

One of the lads came over. He had a bloody nose and cuts and bruises on the side of his chin. "We were attacked by nine or ten lads. They came out of nowhere," he said. "I only recognised one of them; it was James Burgess who plays for Hardwick." The policemen made a note of the name. "We played them this morning and one of their lads got his leg broken by Nigel, that one on the ground," he pointed. "It must have been a group of them after revenge. After the match was abandoned, Burgess shouted to Nigel that he was going to kill him. Will Nigel be okay?" he asked.

"Not sure," replied the policemen. "He is out cold at the moment."

"They all came at us, but it was only Burgess and Nigel who were fighting each other, the whole thing seemed about them."

One of the other lads came over, screaming at the policeman to get more policemen to get off and chase the lads who carried out the attack. The policeman ignored him and waited for the ambulance. He carried on and the policeman had had enough. "I would shut up if I were you, lad," he said. "We are waiting for the ambulance."

"Well, get more police out, then," he screamed.

"I won't tell you again," said the policeman. "Which way did they head off in?"

"Down the Main Street and there's no bus for ages so you should see them," he replied.

The siren from the ambulance could be heard in the distance. The ambulance arrived and the paramedics quickly assessed Flinders and found he had serious head injuries. They attached an oxygen mask and injected him with various solutions and lifted him into the back of the ambulance. They then questioned the other four lads and asked if they needed assistance. They all refused and said they were just cut and bruised and would hobble home.

One lad asked if he could go with Flinders in the ambulance to the hospital, but the paramedic wouldn't allow him to. The policemen established they were taking him to Sheffield trauma unit and said they would go and inform his parents. The ambulance took off, siren blurring.

The police took the names and addresses of the four lads and of Flinders and said they would be in touch. They then went into see Gregorio and took a statement, but all he could tell them was that he had been in the shop.

The police left and drove down the Main Street and in and around the estates for ten minutes, but knew the culprits had a head start and would be hiding. They had one name and they would be able to establish the others, but they would have a drive over to Hardwick after they had spoken to Flinders' parents.

When they arrived at Nigel's house, they were about to knock on the door, when it opened and there stood Mr Flinders. He and Mrs Flinders had coats on and were about to head for the pub.

After finally being invited in, the police told them how Nigel had been in a fight, had been knocked unconscious and was on his way to Sheffield hospital. David, Nigel's younger brother, had come downstairs when he heard the policeman talking in the hallway.

"Come on," said Mr Flinders. "No pub tonight. We better get down to the hospital."

Chapter Twenty-Two

The Hardwick gang ran up the high street as fast as they could. After a hundred yards, James pulled up clutching his hamstring. He felt a tweak in the game that morning and now it had gone.

After two hundred yards, the others stopped to regroup. James hobbled up. "What's up, Budgie?" asked one of them.

"Pulled my hamstring, I think, but I'll be fine."

"Doesn't look like it to me," said Steven.

"We're sitting ducks on the Main Street," said James. "For both revenge from the Kivo lot and the police, we need to get off into the back street and wait for the bus."

"It's not due for 45 minutes," Sean said. "We can be home by then. Besides, all we've done is have a fight, what can the police do? They can't arrest us for that."

He did have a point, but James replied, "The only way is on the main road through Kivo then the lane into Hardwick. It will take us at least half an hour if we run all the way and if they come after us in cars, we've nowhere to hide."

"Them lads were in no state to come after us," Franky said. "What we worrying about?"

They heard a siren in the distance and assumed another police car was on its way. "Quick," James said. "Let's get off the high street until we make our minds up."

They ran around the corner and hid in the alley at the rear of the parade of shops. The siren got closer and James looked around the corner to see an ambulance go past.

"It's an ambulance," said James. "Must be going somewhere else."

After five minutes, Steven ventured out and back and poked his head around the corner to see if anything was going on. He immediately retreated back to the alley when he saw the police car coming up the high street.

"Coppers," he whispered.

They heard the car engine go past and continue up the high street. The bus stop was 150 yards up the road and they now had just over thirty minutes until the next bus arrived.

"If Kivo come looking for us and we're trapped in this alley," said James. "Why don't we check it's clear and then go to the next road off the high street near the bus stop where we will have a clear view in both directions and wait for the bus?"

Sean resented James trying to take control but didn't have a better plan. "Fine," he said. "But it's on your shoulders if it goes tits up. We should have just set off home ages ago."

They moved out of the alley and checked the coast was clear before entering onto the high street. Looking both ways as they walked along, they came to the road off the high street. They were now only seventy-five yards from the bus stop. They grouped together ten yards down the road and Sean chose to be look out. The house had a tiny garden at the front and a three-foot-high brick wall with a privet hedge above. Sean crouched down behind the wall of the corner house. He had a clear view of at least two hundred yards both ways down the high street.

Costas, his four mates and two men from the pub went at a brisk walk along the high street. The other two men had gone to get a car. After ten minutes, the coast was still clear and Sean had had enough. He walked over to the rest of them.

"Come on, you set of pussies," he said. "The bus is here in twenty minutes and I am sick of all this hiding business. They're not coming after us now, so let's wait at the bus stop instead of hiding here like cowards."

Steven and the rest of the Riley mob agreed. James protested and put his argument up again, but they were having none of it. He had no choice but to go with the majority. They walked while James limped into the high street. As they did so, they saw a gang of six coming towards them. They could also make out even from a distance that two of the mob were clearly not lads of their age.

Frank said, "Come on, they'll never catch us." Four of them set off running up the high street. As they did, Sean looked back and saw a car pull up at the side of the gang. The front four kept running and didn't see Sean and the rest turn and head back up the side street.

"We're sitting ducks on the high street," he said to Steven. "Let's get back up the side street and try and lose them up there."

They all set off back towards the side street. James went with them but immediately realised he could never keep up—his hamstring had gone. His only option was to hide and he chose the corner house which, fortunately, was in darkness. He opened the metal gate and hid in the corner. He crouched down and peered through the privet hedge; he could just see four of them disappearing. Everything went quiet for the moment.

The car pulled up next to the six from Kivo and as it did, they spotted the Hardwick lads coming from out of the side street.

"There they are, the bastards," said one of the men.

They saw four run off up the high street and ten seconds later, the rest doubled back and headed up the side street. The two men in the car shouted, "We'll go after them four. You get the ones going up station road."

The car sped off and the rest ran as fast as they could towards the side street. They stopped at the corner to regroup and assess the situation. They looked up the road, but the Hardwick guys were nowhere to be seen.

"Right," said one of the men. "There only options are going up to the end and into the station or right into the White City."

"They won't want to get trapped in the station, so they'll turn right."

The White City was an estate where every house was rendered and painted white. Its other nickname was Dodge City. It mainly housed lower class families who were on the dole or miners short on funds.

"Let's go for the White City. They might not get out alive from there even if we don't catch them."

James knelt down motionless, listening to the conversation. They were on the other side of the wall and his heart was pumping so hard and fast he thought they were bound to hear it. If they clocked him, he was in for the biggest beating of his life. The gang set off and he breathed a sigh of relief. He was about to adjust his position and get more comfortable when the latch on the gate clicked and in came the owners.

They walked up to the step and the woman fiddled around in her handbag for the keys. The lamppost a little down the road lit up the doorway. She eventually found them but on doing so dropped them. They had clearly both had a lot to drink and the man was swaying as his wife bent to pick the keys up. If he staggered at bit more to the right, he would have full view of James kneeling down and any shout could bring the gang back.

The man uttered a few non-complimentary words to his wife and eventually, she picked up the keys and opened the door. As it shut behind them, James let out the breath he had been holding for what seemed like five minutes. He stood up to try and stretch his leg and checked for people through the hedge. The coast for the moment was clear but he was on his own, unable to run and hadn't got a clue how he was going to get home without being spotted.

Chapter Twenty-Three

Franky and the others had only gotten two hundred yards up the high street when the car pulled up beside them. The window went down and the driver scowled at the lads.

"You the Hardwick bastards who beat up our lads?" he said.

"Piss off," shouted Frank.

"Oh, tough guy," he replied. "Well, we'll soon see how tough you are."

It was then a game of cat and mouse for the next few minutes, with the lads ready to sprint off and the car cruising up at the side of them. The car had to stop at one point and the men got out, giving the lads chance to run off again. The men had the advantage of age, height and strength, but the lads had speed. Eventually, the passenger got out fifty yards behind the lads, which stopped them from going back.

The car sped off and stopped fifty yards in front and the driver got out. It seemed logical at the time but proved to be a big mistake. Whilst they had their enemy cornered, they were still outnumbered two to one and 100 yards apart.

The lads stopped and looked in each direction. "Right," said Frank. "Let's run at the one in front. It's four against one and by the time the other one gets up to us, we'll have done him."

They charged at the man in front and he realised their plan hadn't exactly been well thought out. They waded in flying fists and feet. The man caught two of them with good punches but when doing so, he himself was caught by fists and kicks. He was pushed to the ground and several more kicks finished him off just as the other one arrived.

The four turned on him and again, he landed a perfect punch on one, sending him reeling and almost knocked out. The other three exchanged punches with him and when he went down, they made sure he wasn't getting back up.

"Come on," shouted Frank. "Let's go."

Two of the Hardwick lads needed support, as they were hurt and staggering. As they passed the car, one of the lads opened the driver's door and took the keys out of the ignition. He threw them over a wall and they ran as fast as the two injured ones would allow.

Sean, Steven and the other two ran down station road and realised where they were.

The Riley twins had been to the train station at Kivo on several occasions, but they had always been in the back seat of the car and never really took notice of where it was. They knew it wasn't an option to go into the station and so had no alternative but to turn right.

"Shit, this looks grim," said Sean. "This must be the White City."

"We've no chance in here," said Steven. "We need to find a way out."

They kept running, knowing that going back was not an option. They ran past an arcade of shops. Most were boarded up or had metal shutters down for the night. Only one was open: the off licence.

Outside were three younger lads sitting on bikes. They watched as the four unrecognisable lads ran past. The Hardwick four didn't even contemplate asking for directions out of the estate. As they got further down the road, Steven looked back. They were still being stared at by the three lads outside the shop.

"We must be able to turn right somewhere down here and get back to the main road," shouted Trenchy.

The road bent to the right and they spotted a narrow alley.

"Come on down here." They all followed Steven and the alley led to another road. Opposite was a similar alley. They crossed over, went down the alley and came out onto the high street, about two hundred yards from where they had started.

Not wanting to hang around there, they crossed the street, went down a side road, turned right and went along the back of the houses and shops until they came to another side road which was directly opposite the bus stop.

They walked to the end where they found houses with small gardens. "Let's hide in here 'til we see the bus coming," said Sean.

They undid the gate quietly and hid behind the privet hedge. Both ends of the street were just visible through the privet. "Ten minutes to the bus," said Trenchy. "Let's hope it's on time because we are outnumbered and they have two older men with them we might get a real beating if they find us."

"Shut up you ponce and get a grip of yourself," snarled Sean.

They peered through the privet looking for both the kivo mob, and more so, for the bus.

Chapter Twenty-Four

Costas and his gang ran into the White City. It was a rabbit warren of roads; they didn't want to split up anymore so they all made their way along until they came to the shops.

"You seen five lads come along here?" asked one of the men to a group of bikers.

"Yes, a few minutes ago they ran that way. You want us to help you look for them?"

"Yes, please," he said, and the three bikers set off down the road.

The gang passed the alley and looked down. "Come on, let's try down here."

They came out at the next road and looked right and left. They saw the bikers turn into it further down. They put their hands up to indicate they hadn't seen them.

"They wouldn't dare go back onto the high street, would they?" asked Costas.

"Don't think so," was the reply. "Come on, let's try further down."

They reached the bikers and instructed them to check back on the road they had come from. After a few more minutes, they turned right back onto the main street. No one to be seen other than an old couple on the other side of the road.

"What time is the next bus to Hardwick?" one of the lads asked.

"Anytime now," replied one of the men.

The bus stop was on their side of the road further up. "Let's walk up that way," he added.

With that, the bus could be heard coming around the bend. The bus stop was empty, but they kept walking. As the bus approached, four lads appeared from across the street and ran over to the bus stop.

"There they are!" shouted one of the men, and they set off towards them.

Sean heard the shout and looked back to see the gang in the distance. It seemed to take an age before the door opened but as soon as it was open wide enough, they clambered aboard and quickly paid the driver.

"Not being funny, mate, but don't wait for them running up. If you do, there will be chaos."

The driver looked in his side mirror and saw the group of people running towards the bus. He took heed, closed the door and set off.

It was a single decker and Sean and his mates ran to the back and looked out of the back window. The gang were only thirty yards away and clearly visible. They made rude gestures in the window and laughed. The lads, however, didn't stop running. After only thirty seconds, the bus started to slow. Steven ran to the front to see another bus stop with eight or nine people waiting who had just come out of the bingo.

"Listen, driver, you stop for them and that lot catch up and get on the bus and we are dead," he said. "This bus will be wrecked."

"I can't drive off and leave them," he said.

"Well, if you don't, whatever happens is your fault."

The driver looked in his mirror. The gang were still running towards them and he knew it would take a while for the group waiting to get on and pay. He made the decision and stepped on the accelerator. The people at the bus stop looked aghast as it drove by without stopping.

The gang stopped running and watched it drive away. Trenchy and Sean dropped their trousers and underpants and stuck their bare bottoms in the back window.

"They effing got away," said one of the men. "And we were so close."

"The bus driver must have shit himself," said the other man. "To leave this lot standing here."

As the bus went up the street it slowed again to manoeuvre around a parked car in the middle of the road and as it pulled away, the lads looked out of the back window to see the car and two men leaning on the car bonnet. "That's them two blokes," shouted Sean.

"No sign of our lads though," replied Trenchy. With that, they sat beck down with smiles all over their faces.

As the bus pulled around the car, it left the road visible and Costas and his crew could see their two mates in the distance standing by the car. They walked up to see the two had come off worse and then found out they had no keys to drive home.

"The bastards got away," said Costas.

They all pushed the car into the side of the road.

"Come on, I'll have to walk home and get the spares keys," the driver said.

They all turned and headed back down the high street, feeling completely sick. The three lads on the bikes came up.

"Couldn't find them, mate," said one. "We went everywhere."

"Thanks, lads, but they got way I'm afraid."

"Okay then, see ya," and they were off, back into the estate.

"We aren't letting them bastards get away with this," said the driver. "We need to find out who they are and get our own back."

"One of them is a kid called James Burgess," said Costas.

"Has he got a brother called Neville?" one of the men said.

"Not sure," replied Costas.

"I've had run-ins with him in the past. I bet it's his brother. He's a hard bastard."

"The game got abandoned today," said Costas. "I just hope we have to replay it again. We'll kill the lot of them then."

The bus stopped a mile down the road and on got four familiar faces. Sean, Steven and the other two burst into cheers as they saw Frank and the others get onto the bus. They held their hands up in triumph and walked to the back of the bus.

"It's good to see you lot," shouted Sean, "bloody hell. What happened to you, Robbie?" he asked looking at a swelling eye and cut lip.

"Got caught with a couple off that older guy but we got the better of them in the end," he said.

"Where's Budgie?" one asked.

"Don't know," replied Sean. "He hurt his leg and when we ran off, he couldn't keep up."

"The poor bastard," said Frank. "On his own out there."

"We couldn't wait for him. There were about ten of them after us," said Sean.

As they swapped stories, everything seemed exaggerated and when they reached Hardwick, they went their separate ways, feeling like the all-conquering Roman army.

James wasn't given another mention.

Chapter Twenty-Five

James sat behind the wall waiting for the bus in about fifteen minutes. He had no other option. The high street remained fairly quiet with only the occasional couple or single man walking to or from the pub. He had a reasonable view in either direction and when he saw the bus eventually come around the bend, he would have seventy-five yards to limp. His hamstring was getting stiffer by the minute and not being able to stand fully up was making it worse. He heard the drone of the bus's engine in the distance and sure enough, it appeared down the road. No one was waiting at the bus stop and he just prayed someone would be getting off, so the bus didn't drive past. He was about to open the gate when he saw Sean and the rest of the mob about to cross the street.

Oh great, he thought until he heard the shout from the opposite direction. He looked back to see the Kivo mob running towards him and the bus. There was no way he could make it to the bus before the mob caught up to him. He quickly went back into the garden crouched down and hope he hadn't been spotted.

The Hardwick lads came from a garden opposite the bus stop and made it onto the bus. The Kivo mob ran past James in the garden, but the bus was driving away. He could see the lads through the back window and managed a smile to himself, as it seemed they had gotten away. *I wonder what happened to the rest of them*, he thought.

He watched as the Kivo mob kept running, but then they were out of sight around the corner. He knew the last bus through Hardwick was at nine o'clock and that it came through Kivington first, meaning about 8.40 pm here. He had 45 minutes to wait.

He looked again at the phone box near before the bus stop. Should he risk being in the open and phone home for either his dad or Nev to come pick him up? He quickly dismissed that idea. He didn't want his dad knowing what he had been up to and the chances were Nev was out having a pint with his mates or with Karen.

He heard some clatter and saw three young lads go past on bikes. Five minutes later, he heard voices approaching. He peaked through the privet hedge and saw eight of them coming towards him. He crouched down and nearly screamed in pain as his hamstring hurt. He heard them approaching and caught the conversation. He recognised one from the Kivington team and then froze as one said, "One of them is a kid called James Burgess."

As they walked past, another said, "Has he a brother called Neville?"

He held his breath as they passed the garden and stayed there until he could no longer hear the chatter. He Gingerly stood up and looked back to see the gang disappearing around the bend. He looked at his watch. He still had half an hour to wait.

What seemed like ages passed and James stood up in anticipation of the bus. The street was clear apart from a couple who walked up for the bus. James waited until he heard the bus's engine. He slipped out of the gate and limped to the bus stop, looking behind him every few seconds.

He climbed aboard, paid the fare and sat down on the front seat. He breathed a sigh of relief. He wasn't home yet, but surely no one would catch him now. He got off the bus and limped home. He had achieved what he set out to do, but wasn't sure it had been worth it.

He opened the front door and went into the living room.

"Where have you been till this time?" asked his mum. "You've missed your tea and you've got first day back at school tomorrow."

"I know that," he replied. "I was down at Jono's, his mum gave me some tea. He's got his leg broken in two places."

"Oh no," said his mum. He didn't really hear the rest of her conversation and was just glad it was no longer about him being late. He said his goodnights and hobbled upstairs. Alex was snoring his brains out as usual. He went to the bathroom to get ready for bed and then laid down in agony.

As he lay in bed, he thought,

If only I had passed to Crofty and not Jono.

If only then Jono wouldn't be in hospital and I wouldn't have had to go through that ordeal tonight.

If only I hadn't passed to Jono, my leg wouldn't be hurting like this.

It wasn't long before he nodded off.

Chapter Twenty-Six

The next morning, James' hamstring still hurt. Last night, he was so tired when he got to bed not even the pain could keep him awake.

"Alex," he said. "Get up. Get ready." Alex turned over as James struggled to lift himself up.

"What's up with you?" he asked.

"Pulled my hamstring last night—it's killing me."

"Sounds like a day off school to me."

"No way," said James. "I've got my o-levels in six weeks. I can't afford any time off. Poor Jono will be though, he broke his leg in two places, not one and I can't see him being back at school this term."

James hobbled to the bathroom. Every step was agony. The hobbling around made him late, so he had no time for breakfast.

He managed to leave and when he finally made it to the bus stop, fortunately it hadn't arrived. He was about to go into the newsagents to get a chocolate bar—something he didn't normally do, but he was starving—when Sean came running over.

"What happened to you last night?" he asked.

"More like what happened to you lot," replied James.

"It's a long story. Go in and get what you want then we will swap stories on the bus."

James limped into the newsagents. There was a small queue that James joined after he had chosen a toffee crisp.

Frank was in front of him. "Budge," he said. "So glad to see you. What happened to you?"

"It's a long story, I'll tell you in a bit."

The queue lengthened and no one seemed to be getting served. Mrs Richardson had moved to guard the entrance door and then Mr Richardson said, "Right, everyone, I want to check what you've got."

Frank quickly fished four Mars bars out of his pocket. He slipped his hand behind his back and whispered to James, "Take these, he won't suspect or search you."

James wouldn't normally have accepted them but maybe due to the help they had given him last night, he instinctively took them and put them in his pocket.

Mr Richardson spoke again. "No one is leaving this shop until you have all been searched." He patted down the first three customers in the queue and then Frank. He then came to James. He patted James' pockets and found four mars bars.

James looked at Mr Richardson, but was speechless. He waited for Frank to admit they were his, but Frank remained silent, not even looking back.

"James," said Mr Richardson. "I can't believe you were going to steal from me."

James wanted to tell the truth, but the words wouldn't come out.

"I'm sorry, James, but I'm not going to report it to the police. I *am* going to report this to your headmaster and your parents. I just hope this is the first time and you haven't been stealing from me for years. Now leave my shop."

Again, James wanted to say something, but he felt if he opened his mouth he would burst into tears. He just took it whilst everyone was there and he couldn't grass someone up, but vowed to return tonight and tell Mr Richardson the real story. Hopefully, by that time, he wouldn't have reported it yet to the school. He turned, brushed past Neil Thomson and left the shop.

Frank came out. "Cheers for that, Budge. If they had caught me and the police got involved again, I could be sent to borstal. James was going to smack him straight in the mouth, but then Fletch and Ginger came over.

"James," he said. "Do you know how Jono is?"

"Broke his leg in two places," replied James. "I'll tell you more on the bus."

As he was about to get on the bus, the Riley twins and four others came and surrounded him.

"Come on, Budge. Upstairs, we can't wait for you to tell us what happened."

"Be careful," replied James. "My leg hurts like hell."

They helped him up the stairs then chaperoned him to the back. They swapped stories but he knew they were lying when Robbie said they had beaten six of the mob up before they got on the bus, he didn't tell them he saw the whole thing, it wasn't worth it. Frank was wearing his bruises like trophies and talked about how they beat up the two older men. The Riley twins assured James they didn't realise he wasn't behind them until they had run to the end of the road and by that time, they couldn't see where he had gone. He wasn't entirely convinced. He told them about how he had been hiding in the garden because he couldn't run anywhere and how he had seen them get on the bus. They all did share a sense of achievement, though as they had, after all achieved their goal, they had got revenge for Jono. James was extremely appreciative of their help. The rumour that Budgie had been caught stealing went around the bus like wildfire, but most dismissed it. "Not Budgie, he's not a thief," most said. When they got off the bus, James was still surrounded by the gang and had no chance of speaking to Fletch or Ginger and as they were in different houses blocks and lessons that day, he never bumped into them.

James had house football at lunch. He couldn't play, but as he was captain, he felt a responsibility to go and watch. He was sat in double maths afterwards when the headmaster's receptionist, Miss Matthews, knocked on the door and entered the classroom. She spoke quietly with the teacher who then asked James to follow the receptionist to the headmaster's office.

"What's all this about?" James asked.

She would not normally have revealed any information, but Miss Matthews had seen James around school and knew of him to be a well-respected and liked person. She told him of a telephone call from a Mr Richardson. James' face went white. He arrived at the headmaster's office and the receptionist knocked and opened the door.

James entered the room.

"Come in, Burgess," instructed Mr Morton.

James stood in front of the desk whilst Mr Morton finished off what he was writing.

"Burgess," he said without looking up. "I confess my deep disappointment that I have just had a telephone call from Mr Richardson, the owner of the newsagent in Hardwick, and he informed me that you were caught this morning stealing from his shop. Is that correct?"

"Yes sir, I mean no sir, it wasn't like that."

"It wasn't like that? You mean you had four Mars bars in your pocket and you don't know how they got there? Did you or did you not have four Mars bars in your pocket?"

"Yes, sir, but—"

"Are you saying someone else put them there?"

"No, sir, but—"

"If I hear one more, 'but' so help me you'll feel six strokes of the cane. Of all the lads in this school, Burgess, I would not have expected this of you. You, head boy of your house, captain of the football team, never been in trouble before, to my knowledge. What on earth came over you, boy?"

"Sir, if I can explain, yes, I had the Mars bars, but I didn't intend to steal them."

"Then why were they in your pocket?"

"No, sir, they weren't mine."

"Well, whose where they, Burgess?"

"I can't say, sir."

"Well, I don't want you to dig a deeper hole than you are already in. If you are trying to say it wasn't your fault, then I'm sorry, but the fact is when searched, you were carrying bars you clearly had no intention of paying for. You're on report for four weeks and no school football for that time either."

"But, sir—" replied James.

"Out, boy, I said I want no more 'buts'."

James turned and walked out of the office without having explained anything. He went back to class and when the bell rang, ending the day, he made his way quickly out, not wanting to speak to anyone. He walked to the bus queue and was immediately surrounded by the twins' gang again.

"Did you have to go to Morton's office?" asked Sean.

"Yes, all 'cos of Frank," he glared his way.

"Sorry, pal," said Frank. "But as I said, I can't take the rap for this or they'll send me away for at least six months."

Steven put his arm around his shoulder. "Come on pal, we helped you out last night. We're all in this together, we help each other out right?" He kept his arm around his shoulder as they walked up to the bus.

James had three of them in front of him and the rest behind so when they got to the top of the stairs, he had no choice but to follow them to the back of the bus. James calmed down and sat at the back with them. To be fair, the banter was good and he did enjoy their company.

By the time, the bus had emptied and he had hobbled down stairs, Fletch and Ginger had already gone. He hung around with the twins and made the decision not to call in at the newsagents and report Frank for being the thief, he had already reported him to the school so hopefully, he would leave it at that.

Chapter Twenty-Seven

James was having tea with all the family when there was a knock at the door. Alex was instructed to go see whom it was and if it was someone trying to sell them something, to tell them to get lost. He opened the door and was shocked to find Mr Richardson from the newsagents.

"Is your dad in?" enquired Mr Richardson.

"Er, yes come in."

He followed Alex down the hall and into the room, he saw the family sat around having tea, "Oh, so sorry to interrupt your meal, it won't take a moment but I have to speak to you about something," Mr Richardson said.

Sheila was a bit shocked as he had never been to the house before. "Are we overdue with our paper money?" she asked.

"I'm afraid it's not about the paper money," said Mr Richardson. "It's about James. This morning, I found him helping himself to four Mars bars." He looked at James as he said the words.

Everyone in the room turned and stared at James.

"I can explain," stuttered James.

"I hope you can, lad," replied his dad.

"I was stood in the queue when you said you wanted to check everyone. One of the lads in front of me passed the Mars bars back to me and I, just for some reason, put them in my pocket. I would never steal anything! I had money to buy the toffee crisp and if you remember, I still had that in my hand."

"Why didn't you say something at the time, when I asked?"

"I don't know, I didn't want to get him in trouble, I suppose."

"And who was it who passed it back to you?" asked his dad.

"I can't say," James replied with his head down.

"What do you mean you can't say?" his dad growled. "You're in serious trouble here and you won't say?"

James remained silent.

"Well, I'm sorry, but unless you tell me otherwise," said Mr Richardson. "I must assume you took the Mars bars."

"I promise I didn't steal them," said James. "But I can't tell you who was going to."

"Well, I assume you know I've reported it to your headmaster."

"Yes," said James. "I had to go see him this afternoon, he's put me on report."

"Oh James," said his mum. "I don't believe it."

"As it's the first time, James has been found doing something like this," said Mr Richardson. "I won't inform the police, but I'm afraid I must ban him from the shop for the next four weeks. After that, I'll be watching you when you come in."

James said nothing but vowed never to go back in anyways.

"I'll leave you to your meal," said Mr Richardson and he left.

James' parents, Neville and Alex looked at him and waited for his explanation.

"Well," said Peter.

"As I said, they were passed back to me as the lad who had them didn't think I would get searched."

"James, you need to say who the lad is," said his mum.

"If the lad gets reported he could go to borstal."

"Has he threatened you?" asked Nev.

"No, he hasn't, but I did kind of owe him a favour."

"What for?" asked his dad.

"I can't say," replied James.

James had never been in trouble for anything before and it was so out of character that they wanted to believe him.

"I think when you've had your tea, you should go upstairs and seriously consider whether withholding this lad's name is worth your reputation."

"I know what you're saying, honestly I do, but I'm sorry. I can't."

"Fine. We'll see you in the morning."

James accepted his punishment and went upstairs. Once Alex had finally come up, he walked into the bedroom and looked at James. "Why won't you tell who actually stole the sweets?"

"I can't grass on him, it wouldn't be right because he did me a favour and he's on his last warning, he could go to borstal if he's caught."

"Well, I think you're stupid because until you do everyone is going to think your either scared of him or it was actually you who stole the sweets."

"You what, don't you dare even think that okay."

James got in bed and thought to himself,

If only I hadn't passed to Jono. He wouldn't have broken his leg. I wouldn't have been late for school and I wouldn't have been in the shop and I wouldn't now be classed a thief.

If only!

James woke the next morning and as he got out of bed he realised his thigh was beginning to ease. When he walked into the kitchen, his mum was making breakfast.

"I hope you have come to your senses, young man."

"Mum, just leave it, I told you it wasn't me so I hope you believe, I will sort it out."

He finished his food, got ready and then made his way to the bus stop.

Fletch and Ginger were walking to the school bus on the Tuesday morning, they had expected James to call for him the previous night, he but hadn't shown so he had gone to Jono's house to find out how he was.

"Looks like Jono's in hospital until the weekend," said Fletch.

"Bloody hell," replied Ginger. "He must be in a bad way, o-levels coming up as well. What a bummer, shall we get the bus to see him tonight?"

"No need. Mr Johnstone said he would take me, you and Budge tomorrow night."

"What's up with Budgie?" asked Ginger. "He didn't speak to either of us yesterday and since when does he knock about with the Rileys? He sat by them on the bus both ways yesterday."

"Not only that," added Fletch. "He got called to Morton's office for stealing I heard—that's never James."

By the time they got to the bus stop, James was already there and in amongst the Riley mob. He saw his mates and was about to walk over when Sean got hold of his arm and started talking. By the time he had finished, the bus had arrived and his mates had got on. He climbed the stairs and saw all the seats at the front were taken so he followed the Riley's towards the back. By the time he got off, Fletch and Ginger had departed for their respective house blocks.

Chapter Twenty-Eight

On Monday morning, Sergeant Garner and Constable Jones were in the Kivington police station filling out the paperwork from the previous night's fight outside the chip shop. They telephoned the hospital and found out that Nigel Flinders was in a coma but stable. An MRI scan had been carried out and it found internal swelling caused by a serious blow to the head, but no internal bleeding.

That evening, they visited the four lads from Kivington and took statements. Each one said that they were attacked by several lads from outside the village and that the only one they recognised was James Burgess, who they had played football against earlier that day. They also confirmed it was James who alone had been fighting with Nigel Flinders.

On Tuesday, they made their way to Donnington high school to make contact with Burgess. They headed for the main reception and asked for the headmaster. Soon after, his receptionist arrived to escort them to Mr Morton's office. She knocked on the door and entered, followed by the two policemen. After the receptionist had left the room and they had introduced themselves to the head, they began.

"On Sunday evening," said Sergeant Garner, "we were called to a disturbance outside Gregorio's fish and chip shop in Kivington. It appears that between eight and ten lads from Hardwick had gone to Kivington with the intention of attacking the boys they had played against in a football match that morning in which one of members of the Hardwick team had his leg broken. One of the boys attacked is now in the Sheffield hospital trauma unit with serious head injuries and currently in a coma."

Mr Morton shook his head.

"A James Burgess was identified as the one who was in direct confrontation with the lad now in hospital and we believe he is a pupil of your school."

"Indeed, he is," replied Mr Morton. "But I must confess this is out of character for Burgess. He is head boy of his house, an all-around sportsman and never been in any trouble whatsoever. That is, until yesterday," he added.

"What happened yesterday?" Jones asked.

"He was reported to have stolen four Mars bars from the newsagents in Hardwick, something he denies being responsible for, but he refuses to say who was."

"We would like to see him on an informal basis with you present, if that would be all right," enquired Sergeant Garner.

"Of course." Mr Morton pressed the buzzer on his telephone. "Miss Matthews, would you locate James Burgess and bring him to my office as soon as possible, please?"

Miss Matthews found James in art class, where she knocked on the door and spoke quietly with the teacher. Once again, the teacher instructed James to follow Miss Matthews and once again, all eyes followed him as he left the room.

"What now?" he asked as they walked across the playground.

"I don't know, James, but two policemen are in Mr Morton's office."

"What, all because of four Mars bars?"

"Sorry, I know nothing more," she replied.

James entered the room and find two policemen sat in front of the headmaster. "Come in, Burgess," growled the head.

There were no spare chairs in the room, so James was beckoned to stand at the end of the head's desk. Sergeant Garner did all the talking.

"We believe you were involved in an attack outside the chip shop in Kivington on Sunday evening. Is that correct?"

"Yes, that's true, sir," replied James.

"In that attack, we believe you singled out a Nigel Flinders, who you deemed responsible for the breaking of one of your teammate's legs. Is that true?"

"Yes, sir."

"Did you know that Nigel is currently in a coma in the Sheffield trauma unit due to serious head injuries?"

James looked up in astonishment. "No, sir. It's true I was fighting with Flinders and he fell to the ground. I hurt his knee to get revenge for Jono's leg, but when I heard the police siren, I left him as he was trying to get up. He was definitely conscious, I promise."

"Well, he's not now, lad. He is in a very serious condition and at the moment, you are our main suspect for inflicting those injuries."

"As I've said, he was trying to get up when I left him, he wasn't unconscious at all."

"Well, first of all, we need a list of the other lads involved."

"I'm sorry," replied James. "I don't know who they were."

"You honestly expect us to believe you didn't know the names of the other lads involved? Burgess, you are in serious trouble. Do you realise that you're looking at a grievous bodily harm charge or, God forbid, possibly murder, if he doesn't come out of the coma?"

James didn't respond as the reality hit home.

"This is no time for protecting your accomplices. We will find out who they are eventually, so you need to come clean for your own good. You're not going to achieve anything by withholding the names."

"It was me who was fighting with Flinders and I know he went down after I hit him a few times, but I didn't knock him out and definitely didn't kick him in the head. I wouldn't do that—I just wanted to teach him a lesson, that's all."

"Burgess, get a grip of yourself," the head shouted. "It doesn't matter what you think his condition was when you left him. The fact is he is now in a critical condition and you are being held responsible."

James looked at the floor. "It wasn't meant to be like this. I just meant to go and get revenge for Jono—not for this to happen."

"Right," said the Sergeant. "We won't be charging you until we have carried out further interviews and see what happens with Nigel, but you need to go home, inform your parents and ask them to contact a solicitor. We strongly suggest in the meantime that you think about the seriousness of the situation and come up with a list of the lads involved. As soon as we have more information on Nigel Flinders, we will be in touch. Do you understand?"

"Yes, sir," replied James.

"Burgess," said the head. "Until the police take the next course of action, I won't be suspending you, but given two instances in as many days, trust me, woe betide you if you get into any more trouble. Is that understood?"

"Yes, sir."

"I should prepare yourself for possible expulsion from school, missing your o-level exams and finishing up in a borstal. Let's just hope this lad recovers, but in the meantime, reconsider revealing the other lads involved. Do you understand?" James nodded. "Right lad, back to your class please."

James turned and left the room. As he passed Miss Matthews, he tried as hard as he could to hold back the tears.

"Everything all right, James?" she asked.

"Not really," he replied. "Everything is going wrong at the moment."

He went back to the classroom and sat at his desk. There was a buzz around the room, speculating why James had been summoned, but no one dared ask. After art, he went straight to English without speaking to anyone and from there, to the playground for the bus home.

On seeing the Riley twins, he made his way over to them. Trenchy was behind walking Robert Armstrong along in a head lock.

"Why don't you leave him alone?" asked James.

"What's it got to do with you?" asked Trenchy. "He's my bitch and he does what I say."

James shrugged his shoulders in disgust. "Listen," he said to the twins. "I've had the police here today because Flinders is in a coma in hospital. I can't believe it, when I left him, he was conscious and trying to get up, so how come he suddenly be in a coma?"

Steven shrugged his shoulders. "Haven't a clue."

"What about you, Sean? Did you see him? You were the last to run away, weren't you?"

"Didn't notice him, mate," he replied. "I was fighting some other kid and when I heard the police siren, I scarpered as quickly as I could."

Trenchy let go of Robert and kicked him up the backside. "Don't forget my money tomorrow," he threatened.

James looked at him wildly. "Do you have to do that to him?"

"None of your business, Budgie."

Sean butted in, as he could see the friction building up between James and Trenchy. "It was you against him, wasn't it? No one else hit him as far as I could see. Maybe he banged his head on the floor as he fell down."

"It doesn't make sense," said James. "He didn't bang his head he was trying to get up when I left him. I'm getting blamed for putting him in a coma and I could end up going to prison if he doesn't come out of it."

"Frigging hell," said Frank. "Is it that serious?"

"I hope you haven't told the police we were with you," said Sean.

"I haven't, but they said they'll eventually find out, so I would be prepared for a visit."

"Well it can only come from you if they do find out it was us, so they had better not. For your sake," replied Sean.

James looked at him and was about to ask him if he was threatening him, but remembered the head's words so he walked away.

"All right, mate?" asked Fletch as James walked over. "We thought you had fallen out with us. Where have you been the last couple of days?"

"Don't go there, I need my mates more than ever. Come on, let's get on the bus and I'll tell you all about it."

As they travelled home, Fletch and Ginger couldn't believe what they were hearing had happened since Sunday night: the fight, the chase and having to hide in a garden, being passed the Mars bars, Morton's office on the Monday, the police visit to the school and the possible murder charge.

They listened with mouths open. They were engrossed in conversation as the bus pulled up and were the last few off.

The Rileys followed James down the stairs. "Just remember what we told you," shouted Sean.

James stopped and looked back. "I'm not a grass, Riley, so don't tell me what to do." James got off the bus and stood there in defiance of the twins and their mob. Fletch and Ginger stood there not wanting to leave their mate, but knowing they were massively outnumbered.

"Don't threaten me," said James. "You might be tough while you've got your mates around you."

Fletch got hold of James' arm and pulled him away. "Come on, mate. It sounds like you're in enough trouble as it is without brawling in front of the shops."

James pulled his arm away not wanting the twins to think he was afraid of them, but deep down he didn't have the stomach for another fight at that moment. They walked away but James was seething. He wanted to have it out with Sean, Steven and Trenchy, but knew he couldn't afford any more trouble.

"Jono's dad is going to take us to the hospital tomorrow night," said Ginger. "You coming?"

"If I'm not grounded," replied James. "I've got to tell me mum and dad tonight about the fight and Flinders being in a coma before the police come around."

"Take it you won't be out tonight, then?" asked Fletch.

"No better stay in and revise. Can't get into any more trouble that way."

They said their goodbyes and James walked home, wondering how to break this latest set of bad news to the family. James waited until Nev had gone to Karen's and Alex had gone to bed. Both parents were watching TV and James walked up and turned it off.

"Aye, what you done that for?" exclaimed his dad.

"I need to speak to you and before you say anything, please just hear me out."

James went through what happened Sunday night through to the police coming to school that day. With each mention of 'police', 'coma', 'solicitor' and 'expelled', a stabbing pain struck his mum's side. By the time he had finished, tears were running down her cheeks.

He specifically did not say the words possible murder charge. "I promise," he said. "When I left him, he was conscious and trying to get up—I don't understand how he can be in a coma."

His mum burst into tears again at the word 'coma'.

"What about your o-levels if you get expelled?" asked his dad.

"I don't know, I can't think straight. It's just a nightmare, I just wanted to get him back for breaking Jono's leg."

His dad shook his head. "Well, let's just hope he gets better and soon, for his sake and yours."

"I'm not sure if I can go to school tomorrow, I don't think I'll be able to concentrate," said James as he left the room.

"Indeed, you are, son. You need to carry on with your studies until this mess is sorted," he heard his dad say as he climbed the stairs.

James lay in bed, unable to sleep.

If only I had passed to Crofty and not Jono, he wouldn't have a broken leg.

If only I hadn't gone to Kivo and started a fight, Flinders wouldn't be in a coma,

I wouldn't have gone in the shop and been accused of stealing and I wouldn't be possibly charged with murder and no one would be hurt.

If only!

Chapter Twenty-Nine

David Flinders hadn't gone to school Monday and Tuesday as he wanted to be there when his brother Nigel woke up. His dad was on the dole and his mum on disability, so they had no other commitments and they hung around the hospital all day Monday, hoping Nigel would come around.

He and his parents left the hospital at 5.00 pm after another long day on Tuesday. They had been informed by the doctor that the tests and X-rays had shown a single heavy blow to the head, probably a kick, that had caused the injury. They called at the chip shop near home and Mrs Flinders went in and gave the order to a young girl behind the counter.

Gregorio came into the shop and recognised Mrs Flinders. "Hello, Mrs Flinders, how is Nigel?" he asked.

"Still in the coma, we've just left him. That bastard kicked him in the head when he was down, just hope they find the lad who did it and string him up."

"I saw it all going off outside," he replied. "I phoned the police as soon as I could. It was mayhem out there, but I didn't actually see Nigel amongst it all."

"Sounds like a load of lads came down purposely to get them," she replied.

The order was wrapped but Gregorio refused her money. "I hope he comes around soon," he said.

Mrs Flinders thanked him and left. She got in the car and told her husband Gregorio had given them food for free and added if she had have known he would do that. She would have ordered a large peas and curry as well as three lots of chips. David was going to laugh but realised she was serious, so he thought better of it.

They had just arrived home when Sergeant Garner telephoned to enquire about Nigel and to inform them that they had interviewed James Burgess that day. He had admitted to being in a fight with Nigel. He hadn't, however, revealed the names of the others involved and they hadn't as yet made any formal charges. They wanted to wait and hear what Nigel had to say when he woke up.

Mr Flinders couldn't understand. "If they knew it was James Burgess who had attacked Nigel, why he hadn't been charged?"

Sergeant Garner said, "Everything's at hand. We're just waiting to gather more evidence before making any rash arrests."

Later that night, they received a telephone call from the hospital. Nigel had come out of the coma. He was stable, but heavily sedated and there was no point in them going back that night, as he was still not able to communicate. They were told it was best to wait until the morning. But that didn't stop them from waking David up to give him the good news.

They all went to the hospital early Wednesday morning and found Nigel awake and talking but still extremely groggy. Once the hugs and tears were over, his dad asked if he could remember what had happened.

Nigel shrugged his shoulders. "Yes, bits keep coming back to me," he said. "I can remember standing outside the chippy and the next thing a load of lads coming from out of nowhere and attacking us. I remember fighting with Burgess, the one who plays for Hardwick, and me going down. There was a terrible pain in my knee and Burgess kept saying something about me not playing football again. I knew I needed to get up before he did anything else. I remember trying to stand up, but after that, nothing. I don't what happened after that until I woke up last night with a splitting headache."

"Sounds like it was that James Burgess to me. The police have told us they have interviewed him but not charged him yet."

After an hour the nurse came in and informed them that they needed to carry out more tests and suggested they leave and return later that day. They were on the way home when David announced he wanted to go to school for the afternoon. He knew he would be a bit of a celebrity with everyone wanting to find out the latest news, so he wanted to milk it for all it was worth as soon as possible.

He arrived during lunch break and sure enough, all his mates were keen to hear how Nigel was, about the fight, and had they caught the guy who did it?

By the time the whispers had kicked in and it gotten around to Costas, he heard that Nigel was in a coma and almost died, but had finally woken up. He also heard that they had caught who had done it and had charged him with Grievous Bodily Harm.

Costas was over the moon. Nigel had come out of the coma and they had caught the guy he'd seen kick Nigel in the head when he was down. Maybe the police weren't that bad after all.

The hospital telephoned the police station and informed Sergeant Garner that Nigel Flinders had woken up the previous evening and that he was available to be interviewed for a limited amount of time that day.

They arrived at the hospital at 2.00 pm on Wednesday afternoon and found Nigel sitting up, eating his first meal since the ordeal. After introducing themselves and informing Nigel that they had taken several witness statements, they asked if he was able to remember what happened on the Sunday evening.

Nigel proceeded to give the police his recollection of Sunday night's events. He ended with, "I was only fighting with James Burgess. No one else as far as I can remember was involved."

After he had finished, the Sergeant wanted confirmation. "Are you sure no one else hit or kicked you?"

"I'm sure," replied Nigel. "Oh, and another thing, when we were leaving the pitch after that lad broke his leg, Burgess shouted that he was going to kill me. You're not going to let him get away with this, are you?" he asked.

"Don't worry, we'll take the appropriate action." The police officer said, and then thanked Nigel and asked him to contact them if he remembered any more details. Then their business was done and they left.

Chapter Thirty

James arrived home from school, pleased he had survived the day without being summoned to Morton's office. As he walked into the room, his mum informed him that there was a letter on top of the sideboard for him.

He quickly grabbed it and looked at the envelope to see it had a Leeds stamp mark and when he turned it over, he noticed it had four words of scribble on the back, strange he thought but then made his way up to his bedroom and sat down on the bed. He opened the envelope to find four pieces of paper written on both sides and the first thing that struck him was how neat Clare's writing was.

She wrote how she had loved meeting James and the boys, what a great time they had, all about how she loved their time at the club and the barbecue. She said how she would love to meet up again on the summer and sarcastically wrote how she hoped he could find time between his professional football career to write back and finished with three kisses.

James read the letter again and then put it under a pile of shirts in his drawer so it was well out of sight from Alex. *I will write back later tonight,* he thought.

He completed his homework and asked if it would be all right if, after tea, he went to the hospital with Mr Johnstone to see Jono. His dad agreed on the basis that he come straight home after the visit, he had pre-empted this by agreeing to call for Fletch after tea and then they would go to Jono's house to go to the hospital.

They were in the middle of the surplus meat and potato pie from school Sheila had brought home when there was a knock at the door. They all looked at each other.

"Oh no, not again," said Peter, putting his knife and fork down. "Go on, Alex, see who it is."

"Why is it always me?" he asked.

His dad gave him a look that didn't need a verbal response. James sat there, awash in dread.

Two policemen entered the room and apologised to Mr and Mrs Burgess for coming at an inappropriate time, but they needed to speak with them and James.

Nev quickly finished the last forkful and left. Alex took his plate and went upstairs.

"Mr and Mrs Burgess, we assume you are familiar with what happened on Sunday night."

They both agreed.

"Well, we have good news and bad news," began the Sergeant. "Firstly, we are pleased to say that Nigel Flinders gained consciousness last night and we have visited him in hospital this afternoon. He's making good progress but won't be able to leave for a couple of days."

"Oh, thank goodness," said Mrs Burgess, clasping her hands.

"However," continued the policeman. "We have taken a statement from him this afternoon and he confirms that only James was involved in the fight and that it is his recollection that it must have been you who caused his serious head injury."

James shook his head. "He was fine when I left him, he was conscious and trying to get up. I keep saying it, but it's true."

"Well, I'm afraid that might have been the case. But sometimes a punch or kick to the head does not have an immediate effect. It may be that he lost consciousness sometime after you left, without anyone else's intervention."

"What does this mean?" asked Peter. "Are you going to charge James?"

"We need him to come to the station. We suggest you accompany him, along with a solicitor. The charge at the present moment is grievous bodily harm, as James went looking for Nigel with the sole intent of seriously injuring him. We have statements from two people that you shouted to Nigel after the game that you were going to kill him. Is that true?"

"Yes, I did shout that, but it was only said in the heat of the moment, I swear. I didn't mean it!"

Both police officers looked at James but didn't pass any further comment. "We will allow you two days to sort out your solicitor and will see you at Kivington station on Monday morning. In the meantime, we need the names of the other lads who accompanied you on that night. Are you now willing to give those names to us? We have several suspects and will be visiting them over the coming days, whether you reveal their names or not. It would be better for you if you did."

156

"Let me think about it," said James.

"As I said," replied Sergeant Garner. "Several lads of your age from Hardwick are known to us and have previous forms with stealing and fighting. We will be interviewing them in the near future. We strongly suggest you bring that list with you on Monday. You are in serious trouble here, and at the moment, you're not helping yourself. Are we clear?"

James nodded and lowered his head.

The Sergeant asked Mr Burgess for a word outside and reiterated to him all he had said previously.

James didn't bother asking if he could go to see Jono, so he went into the hall and phoned Fletch to let him know. He pretended he had more homework and went to his bedroom. James went upstairs and took out his notebook, and wrote, Dear Clare, thank you so much for your letter, it came at a time when I needed to hear something nice. He didn't go into details but he told her how he wasn't in a good place at the moment and how he wished she lived closer so they could meet up. It wasn't the most sentimental of letters but then it was the first 'love letter' he had ever written. He had already taken an envelope form the sideboard and he wrote her address and sealed it ready to post in the morning. As he was barred from the shop, he would have to get one of his mates to buy him a stamp.

Alex came up to bed and normally would have been full of beans, but he lay on his bed and looked at James as he came into the room. His brother had fallen off his pedestal, fighting, stealing, whatever else.

"Don't give me that look," said James. "It's not my fault. All this shit is not down to me."

"Well, the best thing you can do is tell the police who did do it, then."

"I don't know how he got in a coma! And Frank Docherty stole the Mars bars and handed them to me. I, like an idiot, put them in my pocket, not thinking I'd bloody get checked."

"Tell the police that, then."

"Oh yes, and I am sure Docherty is going to admit he gave them to me."

"You're not scared of that lot, are you?"

"Are you kidding?"

"No way—I'm not protecting them at all, but at the moment I don't know what happened to Flinders. He's come out of the coma and thinks it was I who gave him the blow to the head. Anyway, I'm not talking about it. I've got homework to do."

Alex went downstairs and when he came back up, James pretended to be asleep. He lay there trying to nod off, but the same thoughts kept returning.

If only I hadn't passed to Jono he wouldn't have a broken leg.

If only I hadn't accepted the Mars bars, I wouldn't be classed as a thief.

If only I hadn't met the Riley twins, I wouldn't be looking at possibly going to borstal. It surely can't get worse than this,

If only.

He finally went to sleep with tears on his cheek.

Chapter Thirty-One

Jono was in bed in Sheffield hospital, eagerly awaiting the arrival of his parents and his mates, James and Fletch. His leg had a metal frame around it, so the blankets didn't press down and he was to have a pot on the next day. The operation had been a success. They had inserted a metal rod in his leg, due to the double fracture.

As it was, only two visitors at a time Mr and Mrs Johnstone went in first. After asking how he was and his mum fussing around making his bed comfier Mr Johnstone took out an envelope and handed it to Michael. "This came for you today, son."

"Oh, thanks," Michael replied looking at the post mark and then putting into his drawer.

"Aren't you going to open it?" asked his mum.

"I'll leave it until later, it will give me something to read when you're gone."

After a while, Mrs Johnstone informed Michael that James couldn't make it and that Neil had come in his place. This surprised Michael but he thought James would have had a good reason not to come and see him.

"Right, we will let Ryan and Neil them come in for a bit," said his dad.

The two lads came around the corner and walked over to the bed.

"Jesus!" exclaimed Fletch. "That looks painful." He pointed at the contraption around his leg.

"Well, it was, but it's getting easier. The eight pills a day help, that's for sure. Where's James?"

"It's a long story," replied Ginger. "He was supposed to come, but he phoned Fletch to say he couldn't come."

"Things aren't going well for him at the moment," added Fletch.

They then gave him the abbreviated version of the events from Sunday, they finished with, "we assume he is grounded and that's why he isn't here."

Fletch tried to brighten things up. "I got a letter from Becky this morning, she loves me and can't wait to meet up again."

Jono got the letter from his drawer and proudly showed them, "I hope they all posted one together and James got one, too, sounds like he could do with a bit of good news."

"When you coming home?" asked Fletch.

"Not sure. I've got physio tomorrow morning after they put the pot on and I have to be able to walk with the aid of my crutches before they'll let me go. I need to get back to school as soon as possible for the o-levels, but I don't know if I'll be able to."

After 20 minutes, Mr Johnstone poked his head around the corner and said they wanted a bit more time with their son and the two couples swapped over.

"Well," said Mr Johnstone. "I don't think it would be sensible for you to go on the school bus so I've arranged to go into work late every morning so I can run you in and we will somehow get you home, even if it means booking taxis every day."

"Oh, thanks, Dad, of all the times for it to happen, it's now."

It was time to go and Fletch and Ginger came back in to say goodbye.

"I forgot to ask you said Fletch, will you be able to play football again?"

"They say I should be able to in about a year," replied Jono.

"Bloody hell, must have been a good operation because you couldn't play before."

Jono smiled for the first time in three days and with that, they were off.

Chapter Thirty-Two

On the bus to school next day, James told Fletch and Ginger about the previous night's visit from the police and how he couldn't come to the hospital and in turn he was told about the visit to see Jono.

The day came and went without any dramas for James and after saying his good byes to his mates when he got off the school bus he went straight home, he didn't have the enthusiasm to go out into the village that night.

As they sat down for tea Alex broke the ice by saying he had worn the hall carpet out that week and if there was a knock at the door the chances where it was a firing squad for James so he could go.

James just managed a small smile but gave him a scutch anyway for being cheeky.

After tea, James couldn't concentrate on the TV and at eight o' clock, he went to his bedroom and as he lay in bed, the 'if only' items went through his mind again.

Unbeknownst to him, Frank Docherty and the Riley twins had been visited by the police that night. The lads had already envisaged this, given their previous records and agreed that should they receive visits; they would confess to being there, after all, they only went for a fight and they could hardly be in serious trouble for that. They also agreed that they'd tell the police that James Burgess had instructed them that he was the only one who would fight Flinders because he was going to make him pay for what he did to his mate.

The police first visited Docherty's house and then the Rileys and came away with matching stories from all three lads.

The next day at the school bus stop, James arrived to have the whole Riley gang swarm around him.

"Have you grassed on us to the police?" snarled Frank.

"Yes, you grassing bastard, we all got visits from the coppers last night," added Sean.

"I never told them a thing or gave them any names, I swear," replied James. "They told me they suspected who was with me and must have put two and two together."

"We don't believe you, you lying twat! We went to back you up and you dropped us in it like that."

"Sean, I've said once I haven't mentioned any names despite pressure from everyone."

"Well, don't blame us, but we had to tell them what we saw and that you were the only one fighting Flinders so it must have been you who put him in the coma."

They were all getting too close for comfort for James and so he pushed Sean away. "Get out my face or I'll put *you* in a coma!"

Fletch and Ginger knew they were no match for the Riley mob, but they inched closer. Fletch grabbed James. "Come on, mate, the bus is here."

"We're not done with you, Burgess," shouted Stephen. "You frigging grass."

James turned back. "Any time, Riley, you lot may bully the others but just try it with me."

Robert Armstrong watched as the conflict deepened. He had wanted to show his hand, but he wasn't ready for T-day yet. *At least the attention isn't on me for a change*, he thought.

James was in a bad mood for the rest of the day, and although he attended each class, his mind was elsewhere. Not only were the police after him, but he had the Riley mob to contend with as well. They wouldn't just let it drop so he knew he would have to face up to them at some point.

He was striding toward his double maths at the end of the lunch break and about to turn the corner when Robert Armstrong ran straight into him, almost knocking him over.

"What's up with you?" he asked.

Armstrong was heaving and before he had time to say anything, the answer strode around the corner.

Armstrong and Thompson had been to book club that lunchtime and were walking towards their next lesson when they were surrounded by Trenchy and the rest of the mob.

Trenchy as usual grabbed Armstrong and asked were his money was.

Robert had a plan which was almost completed, but he wanted to be the one to determine when and where it took place. This wasn't it so for now, he had to put up with it.

"I'm not paying you anymore," said Robert.

"You what?" shouted Trenchy. "I'm going to rip your head off."

Robert knew if he didn't run now, he'd never get away. He shot straight between the twins and off, eight lads chasing after him like a pack of wolves.

"Get the bastard!" roared Sean.

As Robert turned the corner, he ran straight into Budgie, who was striding towards his double maths at the end of the lunch break and about to turn the corner. Robert almost knocked him over. "What's up with you?" James asked.

Armstrong was breathing deeply and before he had time, the answer ran up to them. James saw the baying mob arrive and decided he had finally had enough. He shoved Robert behind his body, forming a barrier between the bullies and their victim.

"What do you lot think you're doing?" James spat. "You set of tossers picking on someone like Armstrong, do think that makes you look hard?"

"We'll deal with you later," growled Steven. "This isn't anything to do with you, so mind your own business."

"I've had enough of you lot, so this is my business. You want Armstrong?" he yelled, grabbing Robert's arm. "You'll have to get past me first."

Steven, Frank and Sean were three feet away from James' face when Mr Devon came around the corner. The first thing he saw was a circle of lads and James in the middle with his hands around Armstrong.

"You lot get off him now!" Mr Devon shouted.

James kept his grip on Armstrong, never taking his eyes off the twins.

"Get off him now!"

The gang slowly backed away. "It's him, sir," shouted Docherty. "He's the one picking on Armstrong."

"Get to your classes now, before I put you all on report," he ordered. "Armstrong, you go now, too."

"But, sir," replied Armstrong.

"Now, I said. Armstrong, the bell is about to ring."

"Sir, I need to explain something first."

"Armstrong, it can wait. Go!"

Robert walked off, but he wasn't going to let James take the fall. He would go to Mr Morton's office straight after double English and tell him about the bullying he had suffered. He didn't care about the consequences from the Rileys or Trenchy. T-day was almost here.

Mr Devon escorted James to Mr Morton's office. "I don't believe you, Burgess. You were one of the best lads in this school, but now you're stealing, fighting, and after all that, you're bullying Armstrong? I'm surprised at you."

"I wasn't bullying him—I was protecting him from that lot," James said.

"That's not how it looked to me."

"You know what? I don't care anymore. You believe what you want, I'm sick of being accused of things I didn't do. No one listened to me anyways."

They arrived at Mr Morton's and they walked in. Mr Devon explained what he had seen. The head sat there quietly, taking it all in. He looked at James, disappointment emanating from him. "What have you got to say for yourself?" he asked.

"I was protecting him, sir."

"That's not what Mr Devon saw."

"Sir, he ran into me because they were chasing him. I'd had enough of that lot. I grabbed him, but not to hurt him. I just wanted those bullies to see I was on his side so they'd stop hurting him."

"Well, why do they all say you were bullying him, then?" asked Mr Devon.

"I reckon they don't want to get in trouble," replied James.

"You know, Burgess, I'm sick of you claiming nothing is your fault and I've had enough. Stealing, fighting and now, bullying? I'm not putting up with it any longer. I'm suspending you with immediate effect and I'm going to strongly recommend to the board of governors that you are expelled and not allowed back into this school. You've gone from an ideal pupil, head boy and house captain, to a thief and a thug in a week. I recommend you stop hanging around with the wrong people and get your life together. You're a disgrace. Collect your things from your locker and leave the school premises. Now."

James couldn't be bothered to argue anymore. As he passed Miss Matthews' desk, he shrugged his shoulders. "They just won't listen, will they?" he said and left the room.

Chapter Thirty-Three

The doctor visited Nigel Flinders Friday morning and gave him permission to leave the hospital that day. He needed a prescription for his medication and was instructed to stay on bed rest for the next two days. If he was feeling up to it, he could return to school on Monday as exams were fast approaching.

Nigel was not anticipating passing any exams so he had already vowed to have a massive headache on Monday morning. His parents were hardly the type to insist he go to school. He telephoned home to see if they could pick him up as soon as possible. His dad was still in bed, but his mum promised to get him up and said they would be there later in the morning.

Meanwhile, Michael Johnstone had his ten o' clock session with the physio and clearly demonstrated he was capable of walking on his crutches without assistance. Whilst a wheelchair would be his first form of mobility for the coming week, he needed to be able to move around on crutches as a last resort. He was given to all clear to leave whenever he could be collected.

He telephoned his dad at work who said he would leave early for lunch and pick him up around 12.00. Michael had his belongings packed and his wheelchair at the ready when his father arrived. Mr Johnstone listened to the nurse's instructions and made follow-up appointments with the physios and then pushed Michael down the corridor to the lifts. They arrived at the ground floor and walked towards the main entrance. Mr Johnstone decided not to take on the revolving door, but to go through the automatic double doors. He still hadn't mastered the pushing of the wheelchair and was trying to manoeuvre through when he bumped into a woman.

"Oh sorry," he said. "I'm still a learner driver at this thing."

"You need to watch where you're going," she replied. "You just ran over my foot."

Michael looked left and looked into the eyes of Nigel Flinders and his mum and dad.

"That's the guy who broke my leg," he said to his dad, pointing at Flinders.

"You're the kid who got his mates to beat my son to a pulp, are you?" asked Mr Flinders.

Mr Johnstone did not like confrontation so he quickly continued on through the double doors.

"Your mate isn't going to get away with it, you know. The police are going to send him down for what he did," shouted Mrs Flinders.

Mr Johnstone pushed the chair as fast as he could towards the car park. "I'm not staying to argue with that lot," he said to Michael.

"I understand that, Dad. But he broke my leg on purpose and might have put me out of football for life," replied Michael.

"I know, but that wasn't the time or place to talk about that. He's just been in a coma, Michael. A coma. And the last thing you need is to get that leg knocked so soon after the operation."

Michael couldn't argue with that. After several attempts, they finally managed to manoeuvre Michael into the back seat of the car with his leg up.

"Don't drive fast, Dad," Michael requested as they drove away. "I don't fancy falling off this back seat."

Mr Flinders pulled up on the high street so Mrs Flinders could go to the shop. They parked as near to the shop as they could. Costas was walking home from school for his lunch and noticed the Flinders car in the distance.

At that same moment, Sergeant Garner was driving down the road. He saw Mrs Flinders get out of the car and Nigel in the back seat so he pulled over to see how he was.

Costas approached the car and knocked on the car window. "You all right, mate?" he asked.

Nigel opened the door and got out. He shook his mate's hand and said he was okay but still dizzy, and lightheaded at times.

"I heard you were in a coma. What's that like?" he asked.

"I haven't a clue, I can't remember a thing. It must be like being dead. It was weird when I came out of it, though, like I was swimming underwater and trying to get to the surface."

"Well, at least they got the bastard who did it to you."

With that, Sergeant Garner walked over. "Hi Nigel, pleased to see you're out of hospital. You okay?"

Mr Flinders got out of the car to join them.

"I'm okay, considering what's happened," confessed Nigel.

"Have you arrested that bastard yet?" asked Mr Flinders.

Sergeant Garner winced at the language, but answered politely. "He is coming to the station on Monday and we will make our decision then, but at the present moment, it would appear James Burgess is the culprit and will be dealt with accordingly."

"James Burgess," said Costas.

"Yes, he was the one who attacked me," replied Nigel.

"He may have attacked you at first, but he didn't put you in the coma. I saw exactly what happened and it wasn't him who did your head any damage."

"You what?" asked Nigel in disbelief.

"Tell us who did then, because at the moment, he's getting the blame," replied Sergeant Garner. "And as far as we're aware, you were not a witness to the situation."

"I was in the back of the shop and I heard my dad on the phone telling the police there was a big fight outside the shop. I ran to the front and saw James Burgess stood over Nigel through the window. I knew him 'cos we had played football against him a few times. I heard the police siren in the background and then he ran off with the others. Then I saw you we're trying to get up, but a blonde-haired lad appeared and kicked you pretty hard in the head. You shot back from the force of it, I guess, and hit your head against the brick wall, I heard the bang in the shop so you must have hit it with some force."

"Did you recognise the lad who did it?" asked Sergeant Garner.

"No, but I've seen him in the shop before with his twin brother, who doesn't have blonde hair."

"Why on earth haven't you informed someone of this before?"

"Well, I heard at school that you had the lad who did it and that he was being charged with GBH so I just assumed you had caught the right person."

"Well, we know for a fact that twins from Hardwick were involved in the fight, but are you sure it wasn't Burgess who kicked Nigel?"

"As I've said, Nigel was trying to get up and was on all fours when one of two twins came past, looked at Nigel and ran up and kicked him like he was taking a penalty."

"Right, I need you to come to the station at five o'clock today and give a formal statement," said Sergeant Garner. "What's your name?"

"Costas Theodopilas," he replied.

"And where do you live?"

"Above the chip shop."

"Okay, we will see you later." He turned to Mr Flinders. "Well, it's a good job Nigel seems to be okay and the truth has come out in the end. I've got to do a visit in Donnington and then I'm going to call at the school and let James Burgess know he is in the clear after what we have put him through."

"Maybe he wasn't the one who kicked our Nigel," replied his father. "But he was the one who threatened to kill him and brought the mob of lads down here looking for a fight."

"I agree, Mr Flinders, and whilst we won't be charging him anymore, he will receive a stiff warning I assure you."

Mrs Flinders came out of the shop holding a bottle of milk and a packet of Park drive cigarettes to see the group but before she reached them, the policeman was getting back into his car.

Costas shook his pals' hand again and walked off towards home.

"What was all that about?" she asked.

"You're not going to believe it but it's just come out that it wasn't that lad James Burgess who did our Nige it was some other lad."

"How on earth has that just come to light."

"Costas saw it from the shop but he didn't realise that everyone had assumed it was Burgess."

"I hope their family have got money because I've been told we can make a clam for compensation."

"Hey, Mum, that's surely my money."

"You haven't got a bank account son so we will see how it goes," said his dad.

Nigel hadn't thought about compensation but with this news he stated to plan what he would spend it on.

Chapter Thirty-Four

James went to his locker and cleared out his things. He walked out of the school grounds without anyone seeing as they were all in lessons and got the 1.30 bus home.

He sat on the front seat and thought about how he should go about the next phase. He made his mind up that he had to fight it out with the twins and Frank Docherty on his terms, not theirs and the sooner the better.

He didn't go home. He went straight to the garage where Neville worked and found him underneath a car bonnet.

"Hey, brother, how's it going?" James asked.

Nev nearly hit his head on the bonnet at the shock of hearing his brother's voice. "What you doing here?" he answered.

James told him about the day's happenings and how he needed to confront the gang and get it over with once and for all. Nev was well-respected in the area as a hard nut and with him at James' side, no one would dare join in when James confronted the twins.

"Are you sure you want to get into more trouble?" he asked.

"Listen, they think I grassed on them and I would rather meet them off the bus than be looking over my shoulder every time I leave the house."

Nev agreed attack was the best form of defence so he wandered off to find his boss and see if he could leave early, promising to come in Saturday morning and work for nothing. He received his approval and cleaned up. James and Neville made their way towards the bus stop and waited just out of sight. They wanted the element of surprise as the gang disembarked the bus.

Sergeant Garner arrived at the school at 2.40 and made his way to the head's office. He knew school broke up at 3.00, but as he was close by, he wanted the head and James to hear the news. He reported to the office and Miss Matthews collected him.

"I could do with seeing the head before the pupils all leave," he said to her as he took a seat to wait.

Five minutes later, the head's door opened and Garner was ushered in. "Sergeant Garner, not more bad news?" said Mr Morton. "Come in, have a seat."

Sergeant Garner sat down. "I was in the area and needed you to know some important news that has just come to light. This afternoon, I bumped into the Flinders family, who had just collected Nigel Flinders from hospital. A witness to the whole fracas was also there. We did not realise this individual was a witness to the fight. He then informed me it was not, in fact, James Burgess who delivered the blow to Flinders' head, but instead, it was a blonde-haired lad who he recognised from coming into his dad's shop. The witness also stated that this person has a twin brother. We have interviewed those twins already and they have admitted to being involved in the fight."

"Is this witness absolutely sure?" asked the head.

"Yes, definitely. He lives above the chip shop and knows James Burgess. He saw Burgess stood over Flinders, and run off as Flinders was trying to get up—"

The head interrupted. "Yes, that's the story he told me."

Sergeant Garner continued. "The witness then saw the blonde twin come past and kick Flinders so hard he went back and cracked his head against the brick wall of the chip shop."

"The blonde twin is Sean," said the head. "His twin has mousey hair, that's Steven, and they have both been in trouble many times over the years."

"Yes, we're aware," said the Sergeant. "So I'm here to give Burgess the good news and if it's not too late, to see Sean Riley."

"I'm afraid you won't be able to see Burgess," said the head. "I sent him home for bullying this afternoon and suspended him with a view to expulsion given everything that's gone off this week. Having said that, maybe he was telling the truth about the other things after all. With regards to Sean, it's nearly 3pm now and by the time we locate him, they will have left the classroom."

"Well, I will be going to the Riley's tonight to inform Sean of the trouble he is now in and inform him that we will be pressing charges in the very near future. I'll then go around to the Burgess house and inform them of the new developments."

"Thank you for coming to see me with this information, Sergeant," said Mr Morton.

"Not at all, I am just glad the right culprit has been caught in the end."

The bell rang, ending class and Robert Armstrong was the first out of the door. He sprinted to the head's office and knocked on the reception door.

"Come in," came a voice from inside the office.

Robert entered. "I would like to see Mr Morton, please."

"I'm afraid he has a visitor at the moment," Miss Matthews said.

"I'll wait if that's okay."

"Certainly, but I'm not sure how long he'll be."

Robert paced up and down the corridor, but eventually he sat down and waited. He had never been to the head's office before which added to his tension. He knew he had missed the bus, but it was worth it, and at least this way, he wouldn't have to see Trenchy. Eventually, the door opened and out came a policeman.

Sergeant Garner looked at the boy as he came out and it crossed his mind that he didn't look like the type to be on detention.

Miss Matthews entered the head's office after the police officer left. "There is a Robert Armstrong, one of the fifth-year boys, to see you."

"Robert Armstrong," said the head. "Wasn't he the lad who was involved with Burgess this afternoon?"

"I'm not sure, sir, but he says it's important."

"Okay, give me a moment and then bring him in."

Miss Matthews escorted Robert into the head's office and didn't leave, but stood at the side.

"Sir, I need to tell you at lunch time Mr Devon mistakenly accused James Burgess of bullying me, but it wasn't him at all—he was protecting me."

"Why on earth didn't you inform Mr Devon of that at the time?"

"I tried to, but he wouldn't listen. He just kept telling me to go away or he would put me on report."

Mr Morton shook his head. It would appear not listening to pupils was a common theme.

"Another thing, sir," Armstrong continued. "Paul Trench has been taking money off me for several weeks now. It's because I finally refused to pay him that e and the rest of his mob were chasing me. If it hadn't been for James, I don't know what would have happened. He stood up to all of them to protect me."

"Okay, lad, thank you for letting me know. I'll deal with Trench on Monday."

Robert was leaving when he heard the head say, "Well, if he was innocent of kicking that lad unconscious and bullying, that just leaves the theft of the Mars bars."

Robert stopped and turned back. "That wasn't James either, sir."

"You what boy, how on earth do you know that?" Mr Morton demanded.

My friend, Neil Thompson, was stood behind James in the queue and a lad called Frank Docherty took the Mars bars and when Mr Richardson started to search everyone handed them back to James.

"But why on earth would he take them from him?"

"I am not sure, sir, he just put them in his pocket, but according to Neil, he didn't want to and then he didn't tell as he didn't want Frank to get in trouble."

"He should have said something at the time, the moment it happened."

"James wouldn't steal anything sir, I swear it."

"Right. Miss Matthews, can you get me the address for James Burgess please? I need to go around to his house when I finish up here and set the record straight before anything else gets lost in translation."

Miss Matthews turned and walked away with a big smile on her face.

Chapter Thirty-Five

The Riley gang were waiting to board the bus, constantly looking for Budgie. He was nowhere to be seen.

"He's bottled it," said Sean to Frank as they climbed the stairs.

"Well, he can't run forever. We'll get him," replied Frank.

"That Armstrong isn't around either, the little twat."

As the bus pulled up, Sean met Fletch waiting to go down the stairs. "Tell your mate we can't believe he's bottled it. Missing the bus on purpose?"

"Budgie wouldn't bottle it," replied Fletch. But to be fair, neither him nor Ginger could understand why James hadn't gotten on the bus home. They knew he had been called to Morton's office again, but never dreamed for a minute he would have been sent home early.

"You watch your mouth, Fletcher, or you'll get a smack as well as your mate."

Fletch and Ginger got off the bus and saw James and Neville standing ten yards away. Everyone who had already gotten off sensed something big was about to kick off and no one had started to make their way home. Sean and Steven were first off and soon shut up when they too saw them standing there.

Fletch and Ginger plus two others went up to the Burgess brothers and joined them.

The Rileys were concerned about Neville being there. Sean was the first to speak. "You bottled getting on the bus and now you bring your big brother to hold your hand?"

"He won't get involved unless he has to. It's me and you, Riley."

Sean smiled, looked away and then went for James with a right punch. James ducked and returned two punches that caught Sean clean on. His nose was staring to drop blood and his eye was swelling up. Sean came at him again, but caught two more, this time sending him reeling back and to the floor.

Steven went to make a move, but then saw Neville squaring up so thought better of it. Sean got up, made one more attempt to punch James, but missed and James finished him with an upper cut which sent Sean falling back and into the arms of Trenchy.

"You now," said James to Frank Docherty. "You deserve it for handing me those Mars bars and then not owning up to it.

"Frank didn't have the stomach for it one-on-one."

"Piss off, Budgie. Just 'cos your brother's there to protect you."

James only hit him once and Frank dropped like a stone. He had no intention of getting back to his feet to receive more.

James looks at Steven. "What about you?"

"No, you're all right. I'll leave it."

"You've shit it, more like."

Steven didn't answer.

James turned and walked off, followed by Nev, Ginger and Fletch.

Everyone watching had either experienced first-hand or witnessed the Rileys' horrible antics and finally someone had given them a taste of their own medicine. All it would have taken was one person clapping to cause a roar of applause, but no one dared. Instead, they all smiled and looked at one another.

Unbeknownst to James Beverly Lewis, had watched the fracas and admired him as he walked away.

"Well done, pal," said Fletch. "You were like Muhammad Ali there."

"Well, I feel a bit better now, but after the day I've had, I couldn't feel any worse. Having said that, I've got to go home yet and tell my parents more bad news. It's all gone tits up." He told them about the situation at lunch and about being suspended.

Fletch and Ginger couldn't believe what they were hearing.

"Right, I need to get to Karen's," said Nev. "I'll be back home around 6.30 tonight. Don't say anything to Mum and Dad until I get there. I'll try and give you some moral support. I think you'll need it."

Chapter Thirty-Six

Sheila had finished serving the meals to the school kids and had gone to the staff room to put five spare meat and potato pies in her bag when she saw the headlines in the local newspaper.

'CHIP SHOP BRAWL IN KIVINGTON'. The column described the events of the previous Sunday evening. "Local boy Nigel Flinders was knocked unconscious and eventually came out of a coma Wednesday evening…A youth from a nearby village is helping the police with their enquiries, but no charges have yet been made."

Sheila closed the paper and looked around to see if anyone was looking. She hid it underneath some papers on a table and left before her colleague returned and before she burst into tears.

They were sat around the kitchen table having pie chips and peas when Peter asked what kind of pie it was?

"Meat and potato," Sheila replied.

"Well, I think you should rename it potato pie because I am struggling to find any meat."

"Just get on with it Pete and if you want me to buy pies from the butchers then give me more housekeeping."

"No, no my sweet, its lovely honest."

"I guess that means you would rather have a scabby pie than cough up more money."

James was shaking like a leaf, wondering how to tell them he was suspended and probably not allowed back into school for his exams. He ate and said nothing. Then there was the dreaded was a knock at the door.

"Oh no, who's that now?" asked Peter.

"I told you it's the firing squad for James," said Alex.

James' stomach churned. It was bound to be more bad news.

"Get that," Peter said to Alex.

"You're having a laugh, Dad, it won't be for me."

James gave Alex a look he had never seen before and so he jumped down off his chair. It wasn't a regular occurrence, but he knew he was in for a clip from his brother. He opened the door and found Mr Morton.

"Hello," said Mr Morton. "Are James and your parents' home? I'm Mr Morton, the headmaster at James' school."

Alex froze, he was only ten years old and therefore not old enough for James' school. Even still, he was aware of Mr Morton and his strict reputation, "Err, err, yes they are," he stuttered.

"Well, can I come in and see them please?"

"Yes, I suppose so."

Mr Morton walked inside and followed Alex down the hall. Alex stood in the doorway and announced it was Mr Morton.

James went white. *Oh shit,* he thought. *Why didn't I tell them earlier?*

Mr Morton stood facing the dining table, Sheila and Peter had never spoken to Mr Morton before and had only seen him from a distance on parents' evenings.

I am so sorry to disturb you but I needed to come and inform you and James of some very important news that has come to light this afternoon.

"Would you like a cup of tea, Mr Morton?" asked a very flustered Sheila.

"No, thank you, Mrs Burgess, I won't keep you long but I'm here to tell you that there has been a terrible mistake. In fact, not one mistake, but three. I couldn't allow young James here to suffer longer than he needed to. I hope you don't mind I called on you."

"Mr Morton," said Peter. "It's obvious it's something important so please just tell us."

Mr Morton looked directly at James. "Since I had the cause to suspend you this afternoon." Mrs Burgess gasped and put her hands to her mouth. "No wait, please, until I've finished. I had a visit from Sergeant Garner. You were correct about leaving Nigel Flinders fully conscious that night. A witness had come forward today stating he saw a blonde-haired youth, who he says is one of a twin, kick him in the head, which caused him to hit his head against a brick wall. This is what caused the serious head injury and render him unconscious. So though James committed a grave offense by going to Kivington looking for revenge, he did not directly cause Flinders' coma."

"It was Sean Riley," said James.

"Yes indeed. And then after I spoke to the police, Robert Armstrong came to my office to inform me you were actually protecting him, not one of the bullies, as stated by Mr Devon."

"I did say that, Mr Morton," said James sheepishly.

"Yes, yes, I know, but I haven't finished. Armstrong then informed me that his friend Neil Thompson witnessed Frank Docherty taking the four Mars bars and passing them back to you when he thought he was going to get searched."

"I told you that as well, sir, but you didn't listen or believe me."

Mr Morton hung his head. "I know and I'm not proud of it, but it's unbelievable that these things have all gone against you in such a short time. You must have been going through hell this week, young man. I am sorry for the pain this has caused you, but I implore you to take a lesson from this: Revenge is not the answer. You should not have gone after Flinders that night—that sort of behaviour solves nothing. That being said, I'm pleased to say that the truth has fortunately come out in the end. Now, I will let you finish your meal and I look forward to seeing you back in school on Monday."

He shook James', Sheila's and Peter's hand. Before he left, he looked at Alex. "And when will you be joining us, young man?"

"Next September, Mr Morton."

"I hope you can be as good a pupil as your brother. I'll say good evening to you all."

Peter showed him out and then came back in the room and found Sheila and Alex with their arms around James. Peter joined them. "And we're sorry, too, son, for not believing in you."

"I was dreading telling you I was being expelled," James said. "I was waiting for Neville to come back for a bit of support."

"Come on, enough of that. Let's finish our tea before it gets cold," said Mum.

They sat down and began to eat, but before the second mouthful, there was another knock at the door.

"You're havin' a laugh," shouted Alex. "I'm not going this time. You can, knickers, I've worn that hall carpet out this week."

"Sit there I will go," said James.

He opened the door and saw the smiling face of Billy Steele.

"Gaffer, what you doing here?"

"Just come to give you a couple of bits of good news, James. It won't take a minute."

"Come in, then." Billy followed him down the hallway.

"Hello, Mr and Mrs Burgess. I'm sorry to disturb your meal, but I've just got back from a week in Portugal and I just had to come around and see James."

"It's not a problem," said Peter. "We're used to it now."

Billy looked confused but continued anyway. "Well first, I've received a letter from the league and the committee had a meeting Wednesday night with the referee and, given that the game was into the 70th minute and that Jono was on goal to make it three nil before the foul, they've decided to allow the score to stand. That means we've won the title."

"Get in!" shouted James.

"Second, I'm pleased to say that I've been given the manager's job at Mansfield town. The current manager is retiring at the end of the season and I take over from June. Now I know they're not Liverpool, but they are still professionals and I would like my first signing to be you, James. Obviously, I would want you to continue on at school, but you can train two evenings a week with the reserves and under 18s and if you can't get a lift with me, one of the training staff lives three miles from here so he'll take you. I'm pleased to say that there would be a small weekly wage and appearance money when you get onto the team."

James stood there with his mouth open. He couldn't speak.

Peter stood up and shook Billy's hand. "If you've been away for a week, you won't realise what this lad has gone through the last five days, so this is just the icing on the cake."

Again, Billy was a little confused, but smiled and shook James' hand. "You okay with that?"

James was literally speechless and nodded his head. He had tears in his eyes but managed to hold them back.

"Sorry," he finally said. "As my dad said, it's been the worst and now the best week of my life. Thank you so much, Gaffer, I won't let you down."

"You're welcome. Right, I'll get off and leave you to finish your meals."

He said his goodbyes and patted James on the back. "I take it you'll let all the lads know?" he said.

"I will, and when's the end of season do?"

"I'll give you a ring. It will be after we have had the league presentation and I'll let you know when that is as well."

James sat down, shell-shocked, a tear finally running down his cheek. His dad patted him on the back. "Well done, son," he said. "It's all come good for you in the end." James beamed and began to eat again when the phone rang. "I don't believe!" exclaimed Peter. "Is there no peace?"

James got up and answered the phone. It was Jono to inform him he was home. James said he had some good news and would be around later in the evening to see him.

"Who was it?" asked Sheila. James was about to respond when there was yet another knock at the door.

Peter slammed his knife and fork down. "Not this again," he shouted.

James got up and answered the door. It was Sergeant Garner. "James, we've just called to let you know that." James stopped him.

"It's okay, Mr Morton came around earlier and let me know."

"Fortunately, we came across someone who witnessed the latter stage of the fight and has stated you had left the scene when another lad came past and kicked Nigel Flinders in the head," said Sergeant Garner. "We have just been to see him and he has confessed to kicking him."

"I believe it was Sean Riley?" said James.

"Yes, indeed," he replied. "You are no longer a suspect and apologies for all you have gone through this week."

"No problem it's all over now thanks God, thanks for coming around," James said, and shut the door. He didn't want to spend any more time with the police than necessary.

"Who was that?" asked Peter.

"The police to say they have been around to Sean Riley's and he has admitted to kicking Flinders." James pushed his half-eaten food away.

"Shall I put it back in the oven?" asked his mum.

"No, I'm fine, thanks. I can't eat it anyway. I just feel—" He didn't have the words for how he felt. "Right, I'm going to call for Fletch and go around to see Jono and give them the good news"

His dad got 50p out of his pocket. "Here you are son, get some fish and chips later when you're hungry, you go out and enjoy yourself."

James accepted the money and walked towards the front door almost in a world of his own. As he opened it and went to walk out Nev was standing there about to put his key in the lock. James came to his senses but the look of shock on his face made Nev worried he had already told them and was about to leave home.

"You okay, mate, do they know yet?" he said nervously.

"You will not believe it, Nev, it's been like a football match here but it's all sorted."

He gave Nev a brief rundown of the evening's happenings and then finished by saying, "The biggest surprise is my dad gave me 50p for chips."

"Shurrup, I'm not having that, I believe all the other stuff but not even a crocodile would swallow that one."

Nev took James hand, pulled him towards him and patted his back at the same time.

"I had every faith in you, mate."

James was too choked to answer and walked away but halfway down the path, he looked back and shouted, "Whatever you do, don't have the pie."

As he walked along the road and looked up at the sky. "Thank you so much," he whispered.

When he looked back down, he noticed Beverly Lewis come out of a shop and walk towards him. "Hi James, I was proud of you earlier. It's about time someone gave that bully some of his own medicine. Anyway, what was it all about?"

"Beverly, it's a long story and honestly you will never believe what has happened to me this week."

"Well, if you fancy it, shall we go to the cinema tomorrow and you can tell me all about it?"

James looked at Beverly and then up at the sky.

"What?" asked Beverly. "It's okay if you don't want to."

"Bev, I would love to take you to the cinema tomorrow, but I promise, whatever we see, the storyline won't be as interesting as mine. Shall I call for you or meet you at the bus stop?"

"Meet you at the bus stop at 2.00pm. The bus is at 2.15."

"You're on. I'll see you then, but please don't stand me up like you did Fletch, will you?"

"I promise." She blew him a kiss and walked off.

Fortunately, she didn't see James blush bright red. He called for Fletch and they set off towards Jono's.

"I'm not telling you what until we get to Jono's, but you will not believe what's happened to me in the last two hours," said James.

"Trust me, after the last five days, I'd believe anything," replied Fletch.

James remained tight-lipped until they were sitting in the living room with Jono. After getting the run down on Jono and his leg, James began.

Fletch and Jono sat there with their mouths open.

"How can everything go so bad and then so good?" asked Jono. "It's unbelievable. Well done, mate, you've been through it. Thankfully it's all come good for you."

"Yes, well done," added Fletch. "Not too pleased about the Beverly Lewis date though, I'm sure she's only feeling sorry for you and she still fancies me."

James laughed out loud. Something only yesterday he thought he would never do again.

James lay in bed that night, looking at the ceiling and listening to Alex snoring but wearing a grin that wouldn't seem to go away.

"How can everything go so wrong and then so right, it must be that your life is mapped out from the time you are born and everything happens for a reason."

If none of those things hadn't happened, I wouldn't have been passing the shop when Beverly came out and I probably wouldn't be going out with the best looking bird in the school.

Maybe everything happens for a reason.

James had the best sleep he had for a week and didn't wake up until 9.00 am the next day. He opened his eyes and waited for the pain he had suffered to come flooding back, but then he remembered and everything was now rosy. He looked over and Alex wasn't there. He got dressed and went downstairs to find his mum in the kitchen and Alex watching TV.

"Good morning," she said. "I bet you feel good today?"

"Best I've felt all week."

"Right, go sit yourself down and I'll bring you a nice cup of tea and a bacon sandwich."

"Cheers, Mum, just what the doctor ordered. I'm starving."

"What're your plans today?" she asked.

"Well, I might see if Fletch wants to go into town to shop. I fancy a new shirt as I'm taking Beverly Lewis to the cinema this afternoon."

"After all you've been through this week, I'm going to treat you to one of those Fred Perrys like our Nev's."

"How much are they?"

"About eight pounds," replied James. "But don't worry, Mum. I've got some left from Skeggy."

Sheila opened her purse and got out a five-pound note. "Here you are," she said. "On me and your dad."

"Oh thanks, Mum. That's great."

As James walked into the living room, Alex turned. "You lucky bleeder, five quid from mum and taking that fit bird out! I can't believe one minute you're looking like going to prison for the rest of your life and the next minute, you're up to your eyes in money and fit birds."

"Two things, young brother. First, do not listen to other people's conversations and second, it's what I deserve after the past week and I'm going to milk it for everything it's got." He sat down with a smile on his face waiting for his cuppa and bacon sandwich to arrive.

He called for Fletch and asked if he fancied going into town to which Fletch agreed. "What're we heading for?" asked Fletch.

"I'm going to buy a Fred Perry like Nev's, taking Beverly to the pictures and I want to look my best."

"What you going to see?"

"The God Father, I think."

"Oh, I fancy seeing that myself, can I come too?"

"If you think we're sitting in the back row and I'm sticking my lips on Beverly Lewis with you sat beside of me, you've got another thing coming."

"I was thinking of sitting between you, to be honest."

James looked at him in disbelief. "You serious?"

Fletch laughed. "No, only messing. You go and enjoy it while you can. She will realise what she's missing soon and come crawling back to me eventually."

"Fletch, my old mate. Move on and get over it, there's nothing worse than jealousy."

James turned and smiled to himself, oh boy, life just doesn't get better than this!

The two lads got the bus and went into town. They looked around the shops for an hour and Fletch offered up some of the most hideous shirts he could find hoping James would bite.

Eventually, James came across a shop with a shelf full of Fred Perry's and after a couple of minutes, he held up a royal blue shirt with white lines around the collar and the sleeves.

"What do you reckon, Fletch?"

Fletch looked over and gave a one-word answer 'crap'.

"That's it," replied James, "this is the one then."

He tried it on, viewed himself in the mirror and decided it was the one.

They got the bus back and as they were parting and trying not to grit his teeth Fletch said, "Have a good time, mate, you deserve it."

"Now you know you don't mean it, but thanks I intend to."

He walked in and Sheila said she would make him a sandwich while he got changed.

James appeared in his blue stay press trousers and his new royal blue shirt.

"Wow, you look like a dog's dinner, really handsome, son."

"Why do you look like a dog's dinner if you look smart and a dog's breakfast if you look rough?" he asked.

"Haven't a clue, son, but you look great."

She sat down at the side of him while he ate his sandwich. "What are you going to do about the girl you got a letter from this week?"

"How do you know it was from Clare?"

"Mum's intuition and the envelope gave it away."

"What the post mark?"

"Ha no, the SWALK on the back."

"Why what does that mean I thought it was just scribble."

"It means she sealed with a loving kiss."

James went bright red and was so pleased there was just the two of them.

"Anyway, how do you know?" he asked.

"Er I have had my moments you know; I haven't always been married to you father."

"I will play it by ear and give it time with Bev, it might not work out."

They arrived at the bus stop at exactly the same time and on the journey to the cinema, James told Bev the story of his week.

"Phew, it will have to be some film to follow that story," she announced, "I knew the rumours about stealing and bullying weren't true."

They enjoyed the film and held hands the whole time.

As they got off the bus, James took the bull by the horns and planted a kiss on her lips.

He walked home in a world of his own.

Chapter Thirty-Seven
Eight weeks Earlier

Robert Armstrong sat on his bed with a bottle of his dad's whiskey and his mum's sleeping tablets. A letter sat at his side saying how he had let them down and he just couldn't live with it anymore.

He had thought of several other methods of ending his life, but they would have not left his body intact and he didn't want to make it any worse than he had to for his mum and dad to see, so he poured a large glass of whiskey and tipped his mum's pills on the bed.

He was about to drink the whiskey and had a handful of tablets in his hand when he heard the back door open and his dad shout up. He quickly hid everything and went downstairs holding his stomach. He waited in the living room while his dad made him a sandwich. He looked at his father and a sense of hope flooded his body. A sense of resolve.

He decided he was going to turn the tables on Trenchy, but for the meantime, he would have to keep him sweet.

His dad came into the living room with a plate of his favourite salmon sandwiches and two cups of tea on a tray.

"Dad, you know the sports shop on the high street near our shop?"

"Yes, son. It's owned by Ronnie Walker."

"I went in last week and they've got a bench, a barbell and weights on special offer. I know my birthday isn't until July, but do you think I could get them now?"

"Let me see Ronnie later, he's had plenty of discounted car spares off me over the years so I'll see what I can do."

"Thanks, Dad. I think I'm going to start on a keep fit campaign."

Mr Armstrong didn't make further comment, but he was aware of the money being taken. Robert was a good lad—his dad knew that there must have been a massive reason for it. He was over the moon that his son was now going to take the matter into his own hands.

Mr Armstrong came home that evening with a bench, barbell, weights and a pair of dumbbells as well. Robert looked in disbelief. "Oh, thanks, Dad. Shall we set them up in the spare room or the garage?"

"I think it would be better in the spare room," he said. "It's a bit warmer."

The spare room had a single bed no one used and a small wardrobe that had Mrs Armstrong's clothes and had plenty of room for a bench. It also had a long mirror on the wall so Robert could see his body changing over the coming weeks.

When it was all set up, Mr Armstrong came in with a big tub of protein powder. "This will help you put on muscle, according to Ronnie Walker," said his dad. "Three scoops per day in milk."

Robert surveyed the apparatus. "No time like the present, Dad," he said as he left the room to get changed into his gym kit.

Robert wasn't small by any means, he was a tall as anyone in his year, big boned but his demeanour made him look smaller and he purposely wanted not to stand out but disappear into the back ground. After 60 minutes bench pressing with 10-pound weights on each end, shoulder pressing with 5 pounds on each end, and bicep curls, he felt like Mohamed Ali.

Next morning, he was up at 6.30 am and did a 30-minute run before coming back and trying some push ups. He was still stiff from the previous night's exercise and only managed ten the first set and eight the second before collapsing on the floor.

For the next four days, he ran and did push ups in the morning before school and after tea, he did weights for two hours.

He was working in his dad's shop on the Saturday morning when he decided to wander down the boxing gym just off the high street at lunchtime. He walked in to find two men in a boxing ring, mirrors around the walls, men punching bags and fellas skipping. The smell hit him like a ton of bricks.

He was surveying the various activities when an old guy with a gruff voice came up behind him. "You here to box or just look?" he growled.

"Just looking at the moment. Can anyone join in?" Robert replied sheepishly.

"Anyone can join in, providing they pay the entrance fee. It's one pound for a day pass or three for the week. Then you get in the queue to fight the fella in the black shorts." He pointed to an extremely large man in the ring who was punching seven bells out of his opponent.

Robert looked alarmed.

"I'm only joking," the man said. "You won't be getting in with him for at least a month. Are you coming in or not?"

"I'm afraid I'm on my lunchtime at the moment. Are you open tomorrow?"

"Yep, 7.30 am sharp."

"Okay, thanks, I'll come tomorrow morning."

"Great. I'm Freddie, I'll see you tomorrow."

With that, he screamed at one of the men in the ring to get his guard up and walked over, not expecting to see the skinny young lad ever again.

In the car on his way home, Robert informed his dad about the boxing gym.

"How much is that?" he asked.

"It's 3 pounds a week," he replied.

"I think I can manage that," said his dad. *Hopefully, it's going to work out cheaper than it's currently costing me,* he thought.

Robert arrived home and had his tea and two hours in his gym and went to bed exhausted.

He was up at 7.00 next morning. He did three sets of push ups—he was up to 20 each set—had his protein shake and set off, jogging to the gym three miles away. By the time he got there, he had stopped three times for a breather. There were only two men in at that time and Freddie was mopping up the flooring.

"Well, if it isn't Smoking Joe Frazier," he exclaimed.

"How much do you want to pay, lad?" he asked.

"A full week, please."

He paid his money and Freddie shouted to one of the men shadow boxing in the corner, "Rembrandt, show this lad to the locker room, will you?"

Robert looked at the man and innocently asked, "Why do you call him Rembrandt, is he a good painter?"

Freddie burst out laughing at the thought of the boxers big hands holding a paint brush. "No, it's because he spends half his time laying on the canvas."

Robert looked bemused.

"The floor of the ring is called a canvas."

"Oh, right," replied Robert, still not sure he got the connection.

Freddie shook his head as Robert walked off to get changed.

When he arrived back, Freddie looked him up and down. "Have you ever hit anything or anybody before?"

"Never."

"I thought not. Let's start you off on the punching bag. Chances are the bag will win, but everyone has to start somewhere."

Over the next four weeks, Robert's regimen was up at 6.30 am, weights for one hour, followed by push ups. After school, he would jog to the gym, do two hours there and get a lift home with his dad. His tea was followed by an hour of homework and then bed. He worked at the shop Saturdays followed by gym and a jog home. Sunday was even more intense.

He couldn't believe the gains he had made as he looked in the mirror. The lean frame was already showing clear development of muscle in his chest, arms, shoulders and back. He was up to 60 push ups a set and was jogging to the gym in under 30 minutes.

Freddie also couldn't believe the skinny meek lad was slowly developing into a strong young man. Robert's reactions and speed were his strongest assets. This showed on the high ball which, together with his eye-ball coordination, were exceptional.

It was six weeks since he had first walked into the gym and Robert was punching the bag as hard as he could. A young lad he had never seen before was shadow boxing in front of the mirror.

"Sorry," said Freddie. "Doesn't look like he's showing."

The lad stopped. "You're kidding. I've come from the other side of Sheffield for this." He looked around for any lads of similar age and weight, but only Robert met the criteria. "What about him?"

"No, he's not ready for you," Freddie replied.

They both looked over at Robert.

"Hey, you, punching that bag like you've got broken hands, fancy sparring with me?"

Robert looked over, not sure if he was talking to him. "What me?" he asked.

"Yes, you!"

"No thanks, not today."

"Come on. I promise I won't hit you hard."

"Pack it in," said Freddie. "He's not ready yet."

"Ready for what? We're only going to spar for three rounds. We're not fighting for a world title. I've come here to box so it's him or no one."

"What do you think, Robbie? You up for it?"

Robert shrugged his shoulders and couldn't believe the words actually came from his mouth. "Whatever, I'll have a go."

Freddie put on his head guard and gloves. "Listen, this lad is one of the best in the area. Just stay out of his way, keep your head down, hands up to protect yourself, and bob and weave like Ives showed you. As soon as it gets too much, I'll stop it, okay?"

Robert was numb and still in shock he had agreed in the first place, so he just nodded. The gum shield went in and Freddie shouted, "Box!"

For three minutes, Luke, the up and coming boxer from a rough part of Sheffield, tried his best to knock Robert's head off his shoulders but the face that was there a second ago, was somewhere else when he threw the punch.

"Time," shouted Freddie.

"Well done," said Freddie. "He's not laid a glove on you the whole round, but there is more to boxing than not getting hit. You're actually supposed to throw a few punches yourself every now and then."

That had been the last thing on Robert's mind. His only goal was to not get hit.

"Go on. This round, when you duck, come around with a right hand and see if you can lay one on him."

"Box!" shouted Freddie.

Again, Robert ducked out of the way of every punch.

Then Luke threw a left, Robert tilted his head back and then came around and laid a punch on his jaw. Robert was so shocked that he had actually hit a person and didn't know if he should apologise. He stood motionless for just a second, which was enough time for Luke to seize his moment and hit Robert, sending him reeling to the canvas.

Robert lay there, waiting for the pain to register, but it didn't. He just felt a tingling on the side of his face. He got to his feet, ready for more. He feigned to the left and landed a punch from the right much harder than the first one he had thrown.

Luke took it in his stride and then hit Robert with a combination of three punches, sending him again to the canvas.

"Break," shouted Freddie.

"He got in the ring, that's enough for your first attempt, young Robbie," he said.

"What? He's never been in the ring before?" asked Luke.

"He's never hit anyone before," said Freddie. "Let alone been in the ring."

"You've got potential then, my mate," replied Luke. "If that's your first time, you're a natural."

Robert beamed from ear to ear and shook Luke's hand. "Thanks, mate," he said. "I really enjoyed that."

Robert lay in bed that night going through every second of his time in the ring. For the time being, he had to maintain the old Robert, but T-day was in sight. It just had to be at the right time and in the right place.

Two weeks later and Robert was bench-pressing 80 pounds, doing 75 push ups a set and his best time to the gym was 24 minutes 30 seconds.

Freddie had taken a shine to him and was coaching him for ten minutes a session high ball, pads and shadow boxing. He also sparred every session with whoever was available, size, weight and age didn't matter. It got to the point where the bigger, the better.

He was on the high ball when one night when Freddie came over. "Robert, we have an exhibition day this Saturday at Barnsley. Our gym versus one over there. Do you fancy representing our gym?"

"What, in a fight?" he asked.

"No in a fancy-dress parade. Of course, in a fight?"

"Do you think I'm up to it?"

"I wouldn't put you in if I didn't think you were. All you need to do is be as aggressive with your opponent as you are with that punch bag. I can see there's a lad's face on that bag and you want to punch his lights out. Bob and weave as you do, but then punch as hard as you can."

Robert thought for a moment. "Barnsley, they're all coal miners and tough as hell over there, aren't they?"

"Fine, no problem if you're not ready yet. We will leave it this time." He walked off.

"Freddie, put me down for it."

"Okay, lad. Be here at 2.00 pm. I'll give you a lift, don't have too much to eat, but drink plenty of liquid, okay?"

"Will do."

Robert went back to punching the high ball with even more venom.

They were having tea when Robert made his announcement: he was to represent the gym the coming Saturday against a gym from Barnsley. His mother gasped. "Oh Robert, no. They're all ruffians over there, you'll get hurt."

"Freddie says I'm ready so I'll take his word for it, he knows best."

190

"What time and how are you getting there?" asked his dad.

"Freddie says I can go with him."

"Do you want me to take you?" his dad asked.

"No, Dad, thanks. You stay in the shop. I'd rather do this without you watching."

"Okay," replied his dad. "I'm sure he wouldn't put you up for it if you weren't ready."

As soon as Robert had gone to bed, Mr Armstrong made a phone call.

Chapter Thirty-Eight

It was Saturday morning and Robert's dad poked his head around the door of his bedroom and told him to have a lie in and take his time coming into work. "Get yourself prepared and in the right frame of mind and then take a leisurely walk to the shop about lunchtime," he told him.

Robert wasn't having it. "No, Dad, I need to take my mind off it I am coming now."

"Okay, let's agree to this, have a lie in, let your mum cook you nice eggs on toast for breakfast because that all you will want to eat before the fight, then come in around 11 o'clock."

Robert froze for a second when he heard the word 'fight' but agreed to the compromise.

He heard the front door slam and he jumped out of bed, dressed in his training shorts and vest. He did 30 press ups not wanting to tire his arms out and five minutes of stretches followed by ten minutes of shadow boxing.

He walked down stairs to find a glass of milk mixed with protein powder on the table and his mum about to serve scrambled eggs on two pieces of toast.

"How do you feel?" she asked.

"I am fine, Mum, just want to get it over with."

"I bet I am more nervous than you," she said trying to make him feel better.

Robert didn't really want to talk and he had all on forcing the breakfast down as it seemed something was blocking his throat but he knew he had to eat something now to give it time to digest.

He finished his breakfast and was finally ready to leave. His mum gave him a look followed by a hug that felt like she was never going to see him again. "Good luck, son, be brave."

"I will be fine, Mum, please don't worry." He knew those words were pointless, it wasn't like he was going for a game of chess.

He took his father's advice and had a slow walk to the shop and then spent a couple of hours rearranging shelves and occasionally taking over from his father and serving customers.

He was just glad no one who came into the shop knew and started making a fuss.

Eventually, the time came around to 1.30pm and he told his dad it was time to go.

His dad shook his hand, wished him luck and then pretended to throw a punch which made Robert instinctively duck.

"Go get 'em, champ," he said.

Once Robert was gone, he packed things away and then put the closed sign in the window.

Robert arrived at the gym car park to find a mini bus and five other boxers.

The air was thick with tension and everyone was hyper with the adrenalin.

They arrived at the Barnsley gym at 2.35pm and the butterflies in Robert's stomach were on double time, what had he let himself in for?

As they walked into the gym, he saw it was twice as big as theirs, had two rows of plastic seats around the ring and the reception committee was made up of tattooed men with flat noses and thick skulls. They looked like they had been carved out of stone and were all solid muscle.

Robert never looked them in the eyes and walked past to the changing rooms, following the rest of the lads from his gym.

Freddie called out the fight order. Robert was on second out of seven fights. He sat there whilst the first fight was going on, hearing the cheers and shouts from the Barnsley audience. The rest of the boxers were going through their routine shadow boxing.

What am I doing? he thought. *I am about to fight some hard kid from Barnsley I've never even met, I can't do it, I don't care what they think of me, this kid is going to knock my head off if I'm not careful, I can't do it, I just can't.*

With that, he heard the bell go to a mass of shouts and screams. Three minutes later, Russ, another boxer, came in with his nose bleeding.

"You okay?" Robert asked.

"Yes, the bastard hit me in the bollocks. The ref didn't give me time to get my breath back and then he caught me on the nose. If I see him or the ref after, I'll kill the both of them."

Robert was shocked by the aggression and venom that came from this young lad.

"Right Robbie, you're up," shouted Freddie.

Robert froze, but slowly walked out, flanked by Freddie and Eugene the gym assistant come cut man. As he climbed into the ring, he was jeered and booed. He didn't notice his dad at the back of the room and that's the way his dad wanted it.

Then out came his opponent, a skin head with tattooed arms to a cheer from the crowd.

Robert turned to Freddie. "I thought you weren't supposed to have tattoos until you were eighteen?"

"I don't think those rules apply around here," said Freddie.

He got in the ring, walked straight over to Robert and looked into his eyes, before walking off, smiling.

"What did he do that for?" asked Robert.

"To see if you're up for it," replied Eugene. "Are you?"

Robert looked around the gym and over to his opponent who had his eyes glued on him. "Yes, I'm up for it."

"Remember Robbie, you don't win fights by not getting hit. Sure, dodge them punches, but you have got to hit him as well."

The bell went and for the first round, Robert moved and ducked and every punch missed. The Barnsley lad got more frustrated each time his fist went to where the face had been, but just like a fly, it had moved before he got near. The bell went and Robert hadn't thrown a punch.

As he returned to his corner, Freddie went mad. "What's wrong with you? Look at him over there, his eyes are glued to yours, he wants to knock your head off your shoulders and no matter how good you are at dodging him, he's only got to land one. Put the face you see when you're hitting that punch bag on him. Just imagine it's the lad you've got it in for and hit him, for God's sake."

Robert hadn't realised that Freddie had guessed his ultimate goal.

The bell went for the second round. Robert walked over and ducked a right, then a left, but as he came up, he hit the Barnsley lad with an upper cut that lifted him off the floor.

194

His dad jumped up and shouted as loud as he could. All the crowd turned around to look at him as it was the only shout in the house.

He looked around and quickly sat down again.

The ref put his hands up and counted the lad out. Freddie and Eugene climbed into in the ring and raised Robert's hands. Robert was more worried about his opponent. As he got out of the ring, he walked to his dad.

"I can't believe you're here, dad."

"Well done, son. That was brilliant. I didn't know you were that good."

"Yes, but what are you doing here, who is looking after the shop."

"That's typical of you, son, you've just won your first fight and you are more worried about who is looking after the shop."

"How does it feel anyway?"

"Scary, this lot wanted him to knock my head off its shoulders and I was worried he would, I do feel good though, it's a great buzz."

With that, two Barnsley men came over, one shook Robert's hand and the other said, "Do you realise you just knocked out one of the best lads in South Yorkshire? Nice job."

Robert blushed and just replied thanks before he made his way to the changing rooms.

While Robert was getting showered and dressed Mr Armstrong ran to a phone box and phoned home,

His wife had been sat by the phone all afternoon chewing her finger nails. When it rang, she nearly shot out of her chair?

"He won, he won, I can't believe it, he won," he shouted down the phone.

Mrs Armstrong jumped for joy and whilst her husband recalled the fight, she had tears running down her cheeks.

When Robert emerged from the dressing room, his dad asked if he would rather go with him or the bus with the others.

"If it's okay with you, Dad, I think I should go home with everyone else, some have won but some lost and it wouldn't be right not to give them some support."

"I agree, it's only right, I will go back to the shop and you come around when you're ready, I've already phoned your mum and give her the good news."

Robert watched the remaining fights punching every punch like he was throwing it at Trenchy.

The last fight was a heavy weight with Rembrandt representing their gym. He lasted until the second round and then a straight jab to his nose sent him straight back landing him on his bottom sat down on the canvas. He was clearly dazed and confused and just sat there until the ref counted him out.

Once everyone was changed and ready, they boarded the mini bus to head back home which was a mixture of winners and losers, sad and over joyed boxers. The camaraderie however was great and it had been great day and even though they fought individually they were still a team representing their club. The banter was great and Robert joined in as much as anyone.

The main butt of the jokes was Rembrandt and how he had just sat there motionless. No one went too far because at the end of the day he was a heavy weight and a punch to a feather weight would hurt.

Freddie looked back from the driver's seat knowing he was safe and shouted to him, "Hey, Rembrandt, I don't know about a cauliflower ears you'll end up with a cauliflower arse!"

The whole bus burst out laughing and carried on even longer seeing he was laughing with them.

Freddie then turned to Mikey in the passenger seat. "Another thing, Mickey, remind me to bring a felt tipped pen next time."

"Why's that?"

"Well, if Rembrandt is going to spend so much time sat down with the soles of his size 12 boots showing we could but Freddie's gym on the bottom of them and get some free advertising."

Everyone on the bus burst out laughing again but it quickly died down when they saw Rembrandt wasn't laughing, in fact he was starting to look very annoyed.

Robert looked around the bus and saw a variety of personalities and back grounds but he felt at home and enjoyed every minute, he couldn't believe how far he had come and how much his life had changed in the past two months. When they arrived back at the gym, he said his good byes and they all hugged each other. Almost immediately, he missed them and couldn't wait for the next day to be back in the gym. Freddie ran after him and put his hand on his shoulder. "Well done, Robbie, I was proud of you today, I thought you were going to bottle it but I bet you're glad you didn't."

Robert smiled. "You'll never know just how close I was Freddie but thanks to you I am a different person now."

Freddie made a mock punch to Robert's chin. "It was always in their son, it was just a matter of getting it out."

I am a different person now he thought as he was walking along; the old Robert Armstrong was history in fact Robert Armstrong was history, he liked the name Robbie better. No longer would he lay awake at night dreading school the next day he was ready for Trenchy but when it suited him.

Chapter Thirty-Nine

Robert trained hard for the next few days, then Friday lunch time came and he was in the far side of the playground with Neil, when up came Trenchy and the mob. Robert stood his ground as Trenchy pushed him. "You got my money?" he asked.

"No, and you're not getting any more, Trenchy. I've had enough of you and your thug mates."

Trenchy threw a punch, which Robert dodged easily, but this wasn't the time or place, so he feigned left but went right and ran off. The mob chased after him shouting. Robert turned the corner and ran straight into James Burgess. James stopped in shock and then saw the mob come around the corner.

He got a grip Armstrong's arm and pulled him close.

"What do you think you tossers are doing, picking on Armstrong? Do you think it makes you look hard or something?"

"We'll deal with you off the bus," said Steven. "In the meantime, his has got nothing to do with you."

They inched closer, but just then, Mr Devon arrived and got completely the wrong end of the stick. Robert went straight to the head's office after class and because of this, he missed the school bus home.

He got changed into his gym kit and jogged home, I *bet they think I bottled going home on the bus*, he thought. *But they will soon find out.*

What Robert didn't know or find out until after T-day was that James was about to eliminate one of the twins.

Chapter Forty

On Sunday evening, Robert and his mum and dad were having his favourite Sunday tea: salmon sandwiches, crisps and a cup of tea. He had worked out and had a good session at the gym. He pronounced himself ready for T-day, Trenchy day.

"Dad, could you run me to school tomorrow, please?"

His dad was about ask what was wrong with school bus, but as this was his first ever request to be driven in, he knew it was for a reason.

Robert arrived at school on the Monday morning, purposely missing the mob on the bus and he intended to keep it that way until the bus home. He waited until they had all got on the bus to go home and then ran up and into the seat next to Neil.

"Where have you been?" he asked. "I haven't seen you since Friday morning."

Robert didn't say much back, he listened intently as Neil was describing the scene on Friday night but he kept his voice low in case anyone heard him. Robert was focused, the bus turned the corner towards the bus stop. Robert took off his glasses and put them in his inside pocket. He was the first one off the bus and he walked twenty paces, turned around and took off his jacket.

Neil walked up to him. "What's up, why are you taking your jacket off?" he asked.

Robert handed him his jacket. "Hold that."

He started to roll up his sleeves, but never took his eyes off the school bus. Trenchy got off, followed by all the rest except for Sean, who was obviously nowhere to be seen.

Trenchy saw Robert and smiled. "You've finally got the bottle to show your face, have you?"

As with Friday night, no one left the area, everyone was waiting to see what happened and the atmosphere was electric.

Trenchy walked towards Robert. "You disrespected me in front of my mates and you're gonna pay," he said. He swung a punch at Robert, but before it had finished, Robert had moved and countered him with a right to the side of the face.

Everyone gasped, as they couldn't believe what they were seeing.

It was finally T-Day and Robert had the time and the place just right. He was not going to finish him off quickly. It was going to be a long-awaited justice.

For the next ten minutes, Trenchy swung, missed and caught a counter punch. After a while, his face was swollen, his eyes blacking and his lips bleeding. Robert had made his point, so finally Robert hit Trenchy with his now famous upper cut and sent him reeling back and to the floor.

James was the first to clap and shout, quickly followed by everyone else watching. Steven couldn't believe what he was seeing so as he saw Trenchy fall, he went for Robert.

Robert didn't have to make a show out of this one, so he took Steven out with one punch. Again, the crown cheered. Robert calmly rolled down his sleeves, took the jacket off Neil, who had stood there for over ten minutes with his mouth open.

James came over and slapped Robert on the back. "Well done, mate. I'm proud of you."

"Thanks, James. You know I went up to Morton's office on Friday to tell him the truth?"

"I know, mate, thank you so much. It all came good in the end."

With that, Beverly shouted over to James. "Come on, wanna walk me home?"

"I'm coming, Bev," replied James.

Robert walked off feeling he was floating on air, the biggest weight in the world lifted off his shoulders.

"Robert did I really just see you knock two of the Riley gang out," asked Neil in disbelief.

"You sure did and from now on things are going to be different."

He was about to reach into his pocket for his glasses but decided against it, he didn't really need them and this was now the new Robert Armstrong.

"Just one thing, Neil, don't call me Robert anymore, from now on its Robbie."

"Oh, okay Robbie," Neil said, not quite sure he wasn't going to wake up at any moment and realise it had all been a dream.

Chapter Forty-One

Billy Steele called everyone on the team that night to tell them the presentation would be in two weeks and they were having a joint presentation with the adult team from Hardwick.

At the bus stop next day, James met up with Fletch and Ginger.

"Did Billy phone you last night?" James asked.

"Yes, he did, I spoke to Becky last night as well and she is coming to stay at ours and come with me to the presentation. She's going to ask Jo and Clare if they are coming too, what do you reckon?" asked Fletch.

"Are you having a laugh, Fletch? How can Clare come down? I'll be taking Bev, you idiot."

"You were all loved up with Clare a couple of weeks ago, I thought you would jump at the chance for the three of them to come down."

"Well, first of all, that was before I got with Bev and second, where will she sleep at our house?"

"I don't know, pal, but if you don't invite her, what're you gonna do when we all go to Skeggy for two weeks? You two will be like a pair of lemons while me and Jono are off with Becky and Jo."

"Just don't invite them down. Get a bird from around here to go with you and don't involve them from Leeds."

"Too late, mate. I've asked her now."

"Just phone her back up and say it's not for couples. She won't be any the wiser."

"So you take Beverly Lewis with you, while me and Jono go on our lonesome?"

"Well, Jono is in no fit state to take a bird anyway. Let's be honest, he is hardly going to be dancing around the dance floor. So, in a word, yes!"

"If it was the other away round, you would say the same thing, Fletch."

"I'll have to consult with Jono," said Fletch.

"What would you do, Ginger?" asked James.

"Mmmm, difficult one. I can see your point of view, Budge. Bring your bird from Leeds here and Bev finds out and she blows you out or tell the Leeds bird you're taking your girlfriend from down here and she blows you out so you're on your own when you go away. I'd just bring your Leeds girl and hope Bev doesn't find out and you've got the best of both worlds?"

"But if Bev does find out, or worse, sees us around here together, and kicks off, I could lose both of them."

"But I can also see why Fletch wants to bring his bird down to go with him," he added.

"Right, I'll do you a deal," said Fletch. "If Jono says he wants to bring Jo down, then it's two against one and you'll have to decide between Bev and Clare. If Jono says no, then I'll do the same, is that fair?"

"I guess so," said James after some thought. "I don't believe it. A month ago, I didn't have a bird, now I've got two and could end up losing both."

"As they say, pal, the path of true love is never a straight one," said Fletch.

"Not when you're involved, putting obstacles in my way, it isn't," James replied. "It was so much easier before I got involved with girls."

"I wish I had that problem, and if I was you, I know which bird I would pick," said Fletch.

Jono had been getting a lift into school each morning with his dad as he didn't want to risk the school bus even though he had become quite proficient with his walking sticks.

They met up with Jono at break time and put the question to him.

"Oh put it all on me, why don't you, so I go to the presentation with Jo, but have her seeing me hobble around on crutches and not be able to get up and dance, plus it possibly cocks the holiday up if we do get to go back to the caravan in the summer 'cos Budge and Bev won't be together. Or I have to go to the do on my own and have to sit there like a lemon when everyone is dancing and having the craic. Well, either way, it's not going to be the same for me with this leg, so I've made a decision. It might be the wrong decision, but at least I've made one."

"Bloody get on with it, will you?" interjected Fletch. "I'm losing the will to live here."

"As I said before I was interrupted, I've made a decision."

"We know that, just let us know what it is," shouted Fletch.

"I'm not going to ask Jo to the presentation. I can go on my own and still have a good time."

"Cheers, pal," said James.

"Twat," said Fletch.

"Well, I was never going to please both of you, so I'm sorry, Fletch, but I've made my decision."

"If you say that once more, I'm gonna kick them crutches from underneath you, I swear. I've got to phone her up now and tell her it's boys only."

"Charming," replied Jono as he turned to Budgie with a smile on his face.

"With that Clanger walked up, did Billy ring you about the presentation?"

"Yes, we were just talking about what we were going as," replied Jono.

"What do you mean, going as?" asked Clanger.

"Fancy dress. Billy did tell you all the team had to get dressed up for a laugh, didn't he?"

"No, I didn't take the call, me mum did, but she didn't say that."

"Well, I'm sorted," said Jono. "I'm going as Long John Silver, easy for me."

"That's a good one, what about you, Fletch?"

Fletch was lost for words. "Not sure, I'll go to that fancy dress shop on the high street and see what they've got."

"Good idea," said Clanger. "Right, see you later, boys, I've got double maths."

As he walked away, Jono burst out laughing. "He fell for it hook, line, and sinker. He's that thick. They're probably only up to multiplication in their maths class."

"Listen," said James. "If he has fallen for it, it would be hilarious if he was the only one in fancy dress, so we need to make sure everyone is in on it. Tell whoever you see to go along with the story and not let on, okay?"

They all agreed and then split up for their afternoon classes.

On the run up to the presentation, the Hardwick men's team had organised a competition to raise money for Jono to help pay for taxis when he needed them to get either to or from school.

They had come up with the idea to have a shave off on presentation night, whereby the names of every one of the players from both squads would go in a hat and then the one drawn out would have to have his head shaved. He could, however, obtain sponsorship and/or pay and opt out, but then people from the audience could bid to keep you in. Only one person was reluctant to enter and that was Banksy with his Kevin Keegan hairstyle, who wasn't going to get his head shaved no matter what.

Having said that, there would be about 36 names in the hat so it would be like betting on number 26 on the roulette wheel. Chances are it wasn't going to come in. He managed to obtain sponsorship money over the next week to the value of £10. If he was drawn out of the hat, he believed this should be enough to ensure he didn't have to leave the night with a bald head.

Chapter Forty-Two

James lay in the bath the night of the presentation wondering if he would get player of the year. All the votes had been handed in before the accident to Jono so there wouldn't be any sympathy votes even though he wouldn't have minded if there had been.

He was quite content having Bev on his arm for the night.

He had borrowed a blue suit off Nev and wore a white buttoned-down collared shirt with it. He splashed on his dad's Brut aftershave and looked in the mirror, mmm not bad James he said to himself.

He shouted into his mum and dad's bedroom who were getting ready and said he would see them at the club as he was going to pick Bev up.

Typically, his dad replied, "If you're there first, son, get the beer in."

"If I am there first, I will be waiting in the car park till you get there you tight bugger," came the reply and with that he was off.

He walked to Bev s house climbed the three steps up to the back door, knocked and then retreated back down. The door opened and Bev came out wearing tight red-hot pants, a white blouse and black high-heeled shoes. Her long black hair looked like it had had the carmen rollers in for two days.

James mouth dropped when he saw her, my god you look unbelievable he said, absolutely stunning.

"Thanks, you don't look too foul yourself."

With that, she gingerly made it down the steps not being used to the high heels.

James tried to give her a kiss on the lips but she wasn't having it in case he ruined her lipstick so he settled for a peck on the cheek. They linked arms and made their way to the bus stop to get the 215 bus to the club and James was praying that all the lads were knocking around the village so they could see him arm in arm with Bev dressed in red hot pants but unfortunately his luck had run out because he never saw a person until they got to the function.

With over 140 guests, the room was going to be full and the evening was going to be packed with awards, a comedian for entertainment, and finished off with a DJ to dance to the latest tunes.

All the team had kept up the story to Clanger that they were all going in fancy dress and had arranged to get to the venue early, so they were there when he made his entrance. He hadn't yet revealed what he was going as.

James was seated with Bev at his side, his mum and dad, Fletch, Jono and Mr and Mrs Johnstone all on the same table.

Fletch couldn't take his eyes off Bev in her red hot pants every time she left the table, neither could most males in the room to be fair.

Every time the door opened, the team would look to see if it was Clanger and eventually, he finally arrived. The door opened and in burst Clanger dressed as the comedian Bernie Clifton riding his ostrich.

The room was in uproar as he ran in and he came to an abrupt halt as he realised, he had been set up. What made it funnier was, as Clanger turned his head to look around the room, he also turned the head of the ostrich at the same slow speed.

People started coming up and congratulating him on his outfit. Clanger was not the sharpest knife in the drawer so as the praise was showered on him and he realised he was the centre of attention, he played along with the role and enjoyed it. He walked over and pretended the ostrich was drinking out of someone's pint and then he let the ostrich give the man a kiss which brought the house down once more.

Eventually, everyone got back to their conversations, but Clanger was going to milk his role as much as he could and he and the ostrich entertained each table.

Straight after the meal, it was the shave off and both squads were called to the stage. Thirty-five lads stood there and Billy had the microphone to let everyone know the rules. Whilst he did this, Tony, the men's team manager, walked behind each player with an electric shaver buzzing away. As he passed Banksy, it felt like the grim reaper was behind him and Tony purposely put the shaver close up to his ear.

Clanger, in his new role as chief entertainments officer, strutted up and down the stage to the amusement of all the audience.

Billy moved along the list, giving each one a number and then the bingo balls were put into a bag. The room was perfectly silent other than the noise of the shaver. Billy dipped his hand into the bag. "Number 18," he said over the mic and then showed it to all the players and the audience.

Banksy went weak at the knees. It was his number.

Tony came up behind him, shaver buzzing in Banksy's ear.

"Three pounds to buy out," said Banksy into the mic.

He started off low, thinking no one would bid to keep him in, surely. A voice from the audience shouted five pounds to keep him in. Banksy looked over in bewilderment, it was the wife of one of the men's team players.

"Six pounds to opt out," shouted Banksy.

Tony kept the shaver buzzing in his ear.

"Seven pounds to keep you in," shouted Peter Burgess.

Banksy looked down from the stage in horror. "Eight pounds."

"Nine," said a man on the middle table.

It was someone Banksy had never met, so why on earth did he want to bid nine pounds to see him have his head shaved?

"Ten," shouted Banksy.

"Fifteen to keep you in," shouted a girl from the back. Banksy looked over to see his girlfriend stood up making the bid.

"Are you for real?" he shouted, almost crying. Banksy was in two minds whether to just jump down off the stage and make a run for it.

"Sixteen," shouted Banksy. "And if anyone bids over that, I'm gonna crack them."

Tony was still behind him waving the shaver behind his head. Billy walked over to him and put his hand on his shoulder. "Sorry, Banksy," he said. "It was all a wind up, I had your number in my hand the whole time and everyone was in on it, even your bird."

Banksy didn't know whether to laugh or cry and just stood there silent, but everyone else in the room were creased up. Laughing.

"Right," said Billy. "Let's have the real draw."

He pulled out number 21 who opted out and after a further two bids to opt out, Frazier, the men's team keeper, decided he would have his shaved. He didn't have much left anyway. Tony did his job and the hair fell to the floor. As well as giving everyone except Banksy a good laugh, they managed to raise £22 for Jono's transport.

It was then time for the awards and it was the under 16 team first. Stubby won club man of the year, which was an award for the one who turns up every week and gives his all, whether he plays or not. Jono won player's player, voted by all his teammates. He made it onto the stage with the aid of his crutches but had to be helped to carry the trophy off.

It then came to the manager's player of the year. Billy paused for a few seconds. "And this goes to James Burgess."

Everyone knew of the ordeal he had gone through recently and no one begrudged him this award. He had earned it both for his football playing and for his leadership. The applause was deafening.

He was then presented with the league trophy and was joined on stage by the rest of the team. Even Jono managed to hobble up once again and take the applause.

The rest of the evening went to plan, apart from Fletch getting pie-eyed. Lemmy had been determined to get him back for the fairground ordeal so he set it up with the barman. He bet Fletch he could drink him under the table and they stood at the bar drinking sambuca shots and lager chasers.

What Fletch didn't realise was that he had primed the barman and he had set up 5 glasses of water for Lemmy and 5 glasses of Sambuca for Fletch.

After the drinks were finished, Fletch started to go green and Mr Johnstone ended up walking him up and down the car park for half an hour in the fresh air, trying to sober him up.

After throwing up in the bushes three times and telling Brian he loved him, Brian ordered a taxi and sent him home.

The comedian Jonny Carroll was as funny as a comedian gets and everyone danced the night away until last orders at 12.00am. Nev had agreed to pick the four of them up at 12.15am but by the time everyone had finished their drinks and they had said their goodbyes it was 12.30am. James, Bev and his mum squeezed in the back of the capri and James wasn't complaining because Bev was half sat on his knee.

"If you want to, Bev, I will drop you off at home first," said Nev.

"No, it's okay. Just go to ours and I will walk Bev home," replied James. He wasn't going to be giving her a kiss in front of his family!

When they arrived home, Nev took the player of the year trophy in while James took hold of Bevs hand to walk her home. As they walked away, Peter was about to shout some sarcastic comment but Sheila anticipated it and knocked him in the ribs before it came out.

"Leave him alone, you," she said, "he deserves some pleasure after all he has been through, it could have been so different and look at them, don't they look so lovely."

"They sure do, like two plums in a handkerchief," Peter said quietly and with a smile on his face.

Sheila gave him another knock to his ribs. "That's our son's girlfriend, you dirty bugger, now come on let's go in and have a nice cup of tea and a biscuit."

Peter followed Sheila up the path and was about to say, "I can remember when your bottom was like that my sweet, but it's more like two bags of king Eddies in a blanket now," but he thought better of it.